Fun with Split Ring Tatting

© 2012 Karen Bovard

Published by: The ShuttleSmith Publishing Company
9102 Poppleton Avenue
Omaha, Nebraska 68124

TheShuttleSmith@gmail.com

ISBN: 978-0-9835441-0-4

Biography and Dedication

As this is my first official book, I would like to dedicate it to my mother (Darlene Dolesh Reuter) and my maternal grandmother (Julia Kominek Dolesh). I grew up an honest-to-goodness 'farmer's daughter' in northeastern Nebraska learning and enjoying every form of fiber art that my mother taught me including sewing, embroidery, crochet, knitting, macrame. Sometime in my middle/high school years I finally got my maternal grandmother to teach me how to tat.

I later learned that my paternal grandmother and grandfather also tatted at some point in their lives. I went to the same one-room country schoolhouse (Good old District #40!) that my father and his father (my grandfather) went to--something that is quite a historical oddity today. My grandfather told me that during one harsh winter when he was a student the teacher taught the kids how to tat when they couldn't go outside for recess. I suppose at that time every family had a tatting shuttle in their sewing basket and that thread was available even in a conservative, rural area. Thus tatting really is a heritage for me.

I really took to tatting in college when I rediscovered that tatting was cheap, portable, and afforded me a way to relax. Later when I was married I found a newly-forming tatting club (The ShuttleBugs of Omaha). It was then that I discovered that my grandparents and I weren't the only tatters in the world! That was also when a whole new world of tatting materials, books, clubs, and techniques opened up to me. Up to that point I had only two Boye plastic tatting shuttles, a ball of size 70 white thread, a few Workbasket magazines and a DMC tatting book. If my husband only knew how much money I poured into tatting that year, he would have been appaled! All those books and resources allowed me to learn and explore advanced tatting techniques that I discovered I had a passion for. I started designing classes for workshops and put my two passions of tatting and motorcycling together to create a tatted motorcycle. Since then I have had the pleasure of teaching tatting locally, regionally, & nationally both in its beginning forms as well as advanced tatting techniques and designs.

I reside in Omaha, Nebraska. I am a long-time Electron Microscopy Technologist in a clinical/research laboratory. This a job that requires steady hands and patience....something learned from years of tatting and needlework.

Special Thanks to Jennifer Bartling--my friend, editor.
Without her support, help, guidance, and belief in me, this book would not 'be'.

TABLE OF CONTENTS

FUN WITH SPLIT RINGS BY KAREN BOVARD

HOW THIS BOOK CAME TO BE

This book is a result of a class that I designed for the 2006 Palmetto Tatters Workshop. The theme of the workshop was 'My Heart Belongs to Tatting', so I designed the hearts. After the workshop, I realized I had several other all-split ring designs from other workshops that I had taught. Then I started playing around with graph paper and colored pens and this book snowballed from there!

At this writing, I have a second book of designs laid out that are based on houndstooth-weave patterns, celtic-inspired designs, and motifs that utilize different colors in one piece. I also have a third book of ideas and designs that utilize additional tatting techniques allowing for more advanced designs and use of colors in one design. These other techniques will include: Split Ring Joining Technique, Padded Tatting, and possibly Single-Shuttle Split Ring Technique.

An alternate name for this book could be 'Fun with Geometrics'. I have always found peace when tatting due to the order and symmetry of the pattern repetition. This is especially true of the designs in this book.

UNIQUENESS OF THIS BOOK AND ITS PATTERNS

--All the patterns in this book are Rings. There isn't a chain in sight!

--All the patterns utilize the following techniques: Regular Rings, Picots, and Joins
Split Rings
Take Off Rings

--An in depth introduction to Split Ring Tatting technique and to Take Off Rings is included.

--All the patterns are Visual Patterns.

--Some of the patterns are motifs, while others are either bookmarks or edgings. My theory is that if you only make 5-6 inches of an edging pattern you just created a 'bookmark'.

WHO CAN USE THIS BOOK AND ITS PATTERNS

Although Split Ring Tatting is officially an 'advanced' technique, it is my opinion that all but the 'True Beginner Tatter' can learn the technique easily with the directions in this book. Split Ring Tatting, like most other 'advanced tatting techniques' is nothing more than manipulation of the basics of half stitches to create double stitches that are then used to create various elements (either rings or chains), picots and joins. It is my theory that once you learn the basics and are comfortable with the Big Four of Tatting (double stitches to create rings, chains, picots and joins) you are ready to learn any 'advanced technique'. It's amazing how simple the advanced techniques really are.

But I will caution that this book is NOT for the True Beginner Tatter.

Defintion of A True Begginer Tatter
-Has just learned the basics of tatting--double stitches to create rings, chains, picots and joins.
-Has only made a few tatted pieces.
-Not comfortable with reading written patterns
-Still needs written patterns to tell them what to do next, such as when to reverse work and the order in which a pattern is accomplished
-Probably has not worked with two shuttles

The tatter who has persevered past the 'True Begginer Tatter' stage--those who have developed an affection for tatting--are what I term 'Intermediate Tatters'.

Definition of an Intermediate Tatter
>   -Is comfortable with the basics of tatting.
>   -Has tatted numerous patterns and pieces.
>   -Is comfortable with reading and following written patterns.
>   -May have already been introduced to and/or used visual patterns.
>   -Understands how tatted pieces are created--can recreate a piece without a pattern by copying it, counting double stitches.
>   -Starting to explore and/or develop their own ways of dealing with thread ends and adding in thread instead of the old-fashioned way of 'cut and tying a square knot'.

Definition of an Advanced Tatter
>   -Probably prefers visual patterns to written patterns.
>   -Has tatted several patterns using Split Ring Tatting, Split Chain, Pearl and Node Stitch, etc.
>   -Knows various techniques for adding in threads, finishing thread ends and have developed these skills in their tatting routinely.
>   -Has used Continuous Tatting Technique utilizing Split Ring, Split Chain, Mock Picots to climb from one round to another.

WHY VISUAL PATTERNS AND NOT WRITTEN PATTERNS

In developing patterns for classes and this book, it became very apparent to me that the traditional written pattern-writing style was inadequate for teaching and understanding how to work my split ring tatting designs. When I did write out the patterns they were very lengthy. Many times each individual ring required its own set of written directions. I also realized that it was difficult to convey which thread sources were used on the various portions of the split ring. I tried writing directions as to which shuttle/thread source to use and again, the directions just became longer and in my opinion more difficult to gain useful information from.

Thus I came up with a visual pattern that shows each thread source in a different color. It allows me to direct which portion of the split ring is to be tatted and in what order.

WHAT IS SPLIT RING TATTING TECHNIQUE?

Split Ring Tatting is the use of both regular, transferred double stitches and reverse, untransferred double stitches in one ring to create ring elements that are connected without any threads, chains or other structures between them. It facilitates exiting or finishing the ring at a point other than where the ring was started.

TRADITIONAL TATTING VS SPLIT RING TATTING TECHNIQUE COMPARISON

To understand the uniqueness of Split Ring Tatting and its effect on tatted pattern design, one must understand the difference between Traditional Tatting Technique and Split Ring Tatting Technique.

In *Traditional Tatting Technique* a Ring is defined by the following characteristics:
>   A. Made with one thread source (eg. 1 shuttle).
>   B. Starts and ends at the same point.
>   C. Made using transferred double stitches only.

In Traditional Tatting Technique one needs either the use of a bare space of thread or a 'chain' element to go from one ring to another to create designs/patterns.

Split Ring Tatting Technique breaks from these limitations of Traditional Tatting technique and allows rings to be created that start at one point and end at another point by use of a second thread source. It is this uniqueness that opens up whole new possibilities that are just beginning to be explored in the tatting world today.

All the designs in this book are unique and could not be tatted with Traditional Tatting Technique unless you were willing to make one or two rings at a time as a round. Imagine the thread ends to finish if you were to do that!

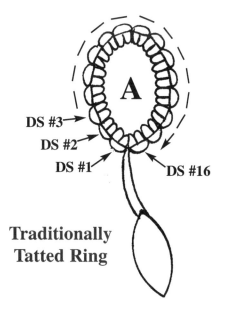

DS #3

DS #2

DS #1

DS #16

**Traditionally
Tatted Ring**

Traditional Tatting Technique

       -Utilizes onethread source (usually a shuttle) to create a ring.

       -The ring starts and ends at the same point.

       -Made using transferred double stitches only.

       -Rings are created in 2 steps:

                1. Forming regular, transferred double stitches

                2. Closing the ring.

Regular, Transferred DS's

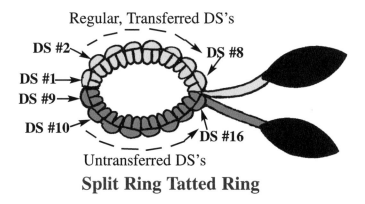

DS #2

DS #8

DS #1

DS #9

DS #10

DS #16

Untransferred DS's

Split Ring Tatted Ring

Split Ring Tatting Technique

       -Utilizes two thread sources (usually two shuttles) to create one ring.

       -Rings start at one point and end at another point along the ring.

       -Made using both transferred and untransferred double stitches in varying proportions.

       -Rings are created in 3 steps:

                1. Forming regular, transferred double stitches using the first thread source.

                2. Forming reverse, untransferred double stitches using the second thread source.

                3. Closing the ring using the first thread source.

Step by Step Directions to make a 5 DS / 5 DS Split Ring

Step 1

With Shuttle A: Form a ring on the left hand as normal and tat 5 regular, transferred double stitches (Under Stitch first, then Over Stitch=one Double Stitch). *ILLUS A*

Drop Shuttle A over the back of the left hand to get it out of the way. *ILLUS E*

Bring the lower portion of the ring thread up so that it lays on top of the index finger. *ILLUS E*

Adjust the the ring thread so that you can comfortably keep tension on the ring for the next steps.

Step 2

With Shuttle B: Tat the second portion of the split ring with 5 reverse, untransferred double stitches on the lower portion of the ring thread (Over Stitch first, then Under Stitch=one Double Stitch. *ILLUS B & C*

Step 3

Close the ring by pulling Shuttle A thread. *ILLUS D*

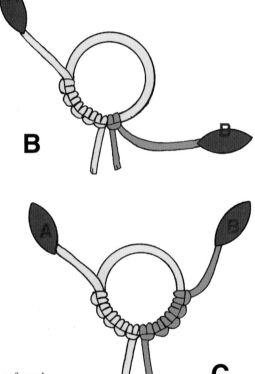

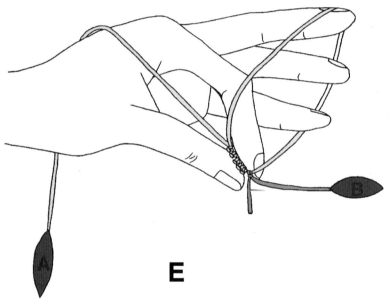

E

A Note about Tension

If you are new to Split Ring Tatting, your tension between the first (regular, transferred DS's) and the second (reverse, untransferred DS's) portions of the split ring may not match. The reverse, untransferred double stitches are a new skill and thus take time to master. With a little practice and experience, you will teach your hands how to tension the reverse, untransferred double stitches to match the appearance of the regular, transferred double stitches.

Written Pattern Directions for Split Ring Tatting

Directions for the previous split ring are written in the following way: **SR: 5/5.**
> -The '**S**' is an abbreviation for 'split' and the '**R**' for 'ring'.
> -The first '5' directs you to tat 5 regular, transferred double stitches. The second '5' directs you to tat 5 reverse, untransferred double stitches.
> -The use of the '/' is a clue that the ring is a split ring.

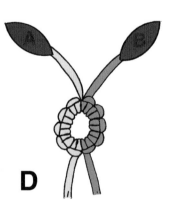

REVERSE DOUBLE STITCH

Historically, the double stitches that create the second portion of the split ring are called "*Reverse [Double] Stitches*" or Lark's Head Knots.

<u>The term 'Reverse' has meaning in two different ways:</u>
1. The individual half stitches are formed as normal but they are not transferred.
    -A difficult aspect of learning Split Ring Tatting technique is how NOT to transfer the reverse half stitches as they are made. For almost all Intermediate Tatters, transferring stitches is something they do without thinking about it. Our fingers are trained to automatically do this. You must concentrate on keeping tension on the ring thread with the left hand. Put outward pressure on the ring thread, never allowing it to slacken. The key to keeping tension on the ring thread (so that the stitches do not transfer) is to keep the ring at a comfortable size for ones fingers. If even one half stitch is transferred, the whole split ring will not close. This is just like not transferring one half stitch in a regularly-tatted ring. There just is no such thing as 99% accuracy in double stitch creation!

2. The order in which the half stitches are worked to create a double stitch on the second portion of the split ring is 'reversed' in relation to the half stitch order of the first portion. This is done so that the double stitch of both portions match in appearance to one another. In other words, are both 'frontside' stitches or are both 'backside' stitches.

<u>Traditionally a double stitch is tatted:</u>   A. Under Stitch--first   *ILLUS F*
                                                       B. Over Stitch--second   *ILLUS G*

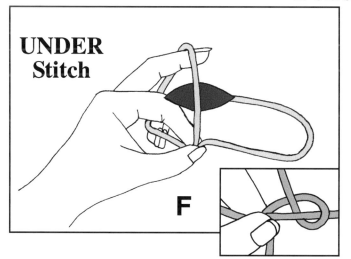

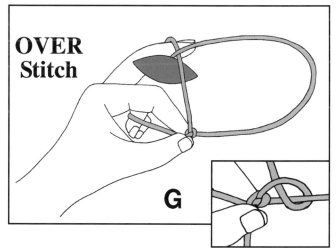

Because the half stitches of the second portion of the split ring are not transferred they are in fact 'reversed' in order. So for a uniform appearance, the second portion half stitches are tatted in 'reverse order' compared to the first portion half stitches.

<u>**First Portion of the Split Ring**</u>
Regular, Transferred Double Stitches
Under Stitch--first
Over Stitch--second

<u>**Second Portion of the Split Ring**</u>
Reverse, Untransferred Double Stitches
Over Stitch--first
Under Stitch--second

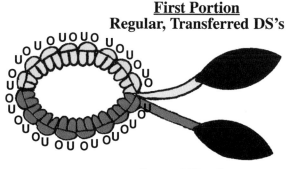

First Portion
Regular, Transferred DS's

Second Portion
Reverse, Untransferred DS's

THREE METHODS TO TAT SPLIT RINGS PHYSICALLY

When I first unveiled my name and idea for this book to my local tatting club as 'Fun with Split Rings' I was confronted with the comment that "...there wasn't anything 'fun' about split rings!" I was shocked to hear this and when I inquired about why a few of my fellow tatters felt this way they responded that when they tatted split rings their fingers would get cramped. This was because the technique they used was inappropriate for them.

The challenge comes in tatting the second portion of the split ring. No matter which method you choose to use, you must be able to comfortably apply and control outward pressure on the ring thread. The key is choosing the correct ring size for you. You may need to shorten or length your ring thread after working the first portion (the regular, transferred double stitches) of the split ring and before working the second portion (the reverse, untransferred double stitches).

There are three different methods to physically tat the second portion (Step B) of split rings. Choose the one that works best for you!

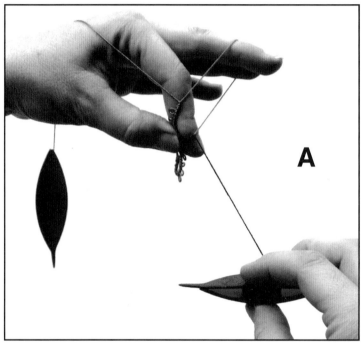

METHOD 1   Bring the lower portion of the ring thread up onto the top of the left hand index finger.
ILLUS A

> *Hint: Slip the L pinky finger out of the ring while working the untransferred reverse stitches.*

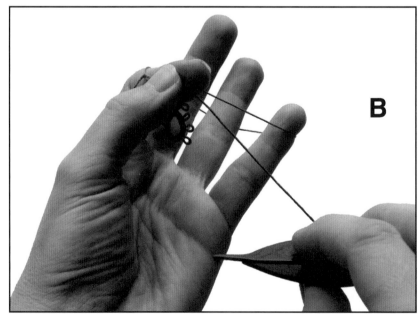

METHOD 2   This is known as the 'Dead Spider Method'

Turn whole left hand so that the palm faces up and the area of thread to work the reverse double stitches is up.
ILLUS B

METHOD 3 Take the ring off left hand. Turn the work so that the last regular, transferred double stitch made is down. Then insert left hand fingers into ring. The portion of the ring thread where the reverse untransferred double stitches will be made will be up.
ILLUS C

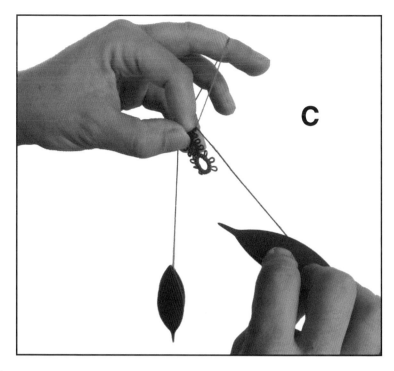

VARIATIONS OF SPLIT RING TATTING TECHNIQUE

USE OF ONE OR TWO COLORS OF THREAD

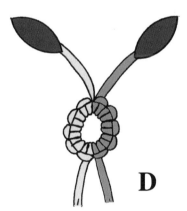

ILLUS D shows a 10 double stitch split ring in which 5 double stitches were made with the grey thread (first portion) and then 5 double stitches were made with the red thread.

However if both portions of the split ring were made using the same colored thread the split ring would look like ***ILLUS E***.

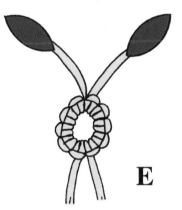

USE OF PICOTS

Picots can be created between any double stitch on either portion of the split ring.

A picot is simply a space of thread between two double stitches.

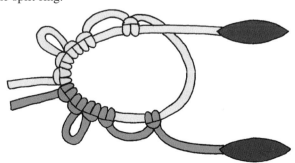

USE OR SPACE OR NO SPACE OF THREAD BETWEEN SPLIT RINGS

As in Traditional/Basic Tatting, unless a pattern calls for 'a space of thread' or 'leave a space of thread' between ring elements, Split Rings are to be made close to one another with no visual gaps of thread or space betwen adjacent rings. *ILLUS A*

However, spaces of thread can be created between Split Rings that mimic picot spaces or joins in appearance. This concept is used in Continuous Tatting Technique to climb out from one round or element into a new round or element. This eliminates starting and ending thread ends that have to be secured (tied into square knots) and then concealed. These picot spaces between elements are known as Mock Picots. *ILLUS B*

EVEN SPLIT RING TATTING

ILLUS C shows a ring that is tatted with 8 regular, transferred double stitches using the grey-colored thread and then 8 untransferred double stitches using the red-colored thread. There are the same number of stitches on each portion of the split ring. This is an example of an Even Split Ring.

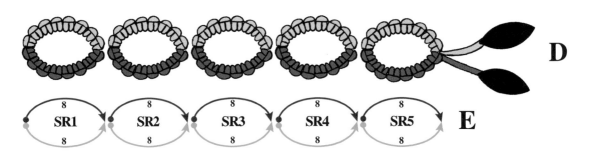

ILLUS D and the corresponding visual pattern *ILLUS E* show a pattern of five even split rings made with two different thread colors for the thread sources.

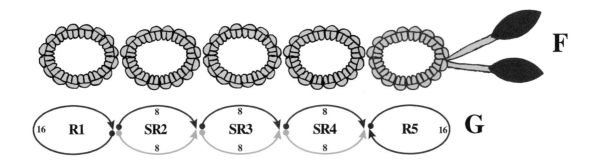

ILLUS F and the corresponding visual pattern *ILLUS G* show a pattern of five even split rings made with the same thread color for the two thread sources. Because both thread sources are of the same thread color, this pattern can be started differently than *ILLUS D/E*. The first and last rings are made with regular, transferred rings, not split ring tatted rings.

Directions as to how to read and use the Visual Patterns are available later in this book (pages 13-15).

UNEVEN SPLIT RING TATTING

Even split ring technique allows one to make straight-line chains of rings. However a world with only straight lines would be a boring one and have limitations to design potential. Split Ring Tatting technique allows us to alter the number of stitches on each portion of the split ring...that is, the number of stitches created with each thread source does *not* have to match or be even.

ILLUS H shows a split ring created with 12 regular, transferred double stitches tatted with grey-colored thread and then 4 reverse, untransferred double stitch tatted with the red-colored thread. This is an example of an Uneven Split Ring.

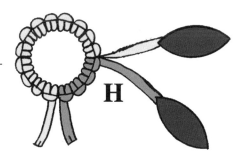

The Following Examples are Forms of Uneven Split Rings

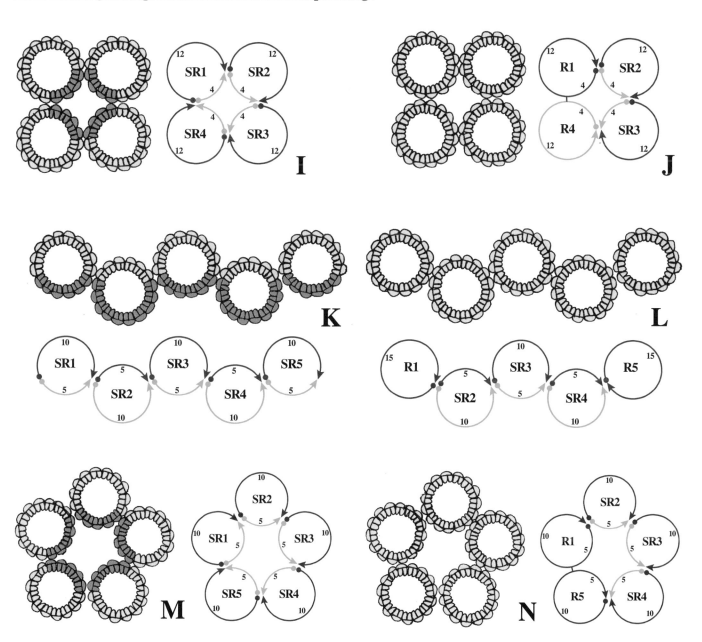

Introduction to Take Off Rings (TOR's)

Also known as Thrown Off Rings. (Uses the same acronym of 'TOR'.)

Take Off Rings are regularly-tatted rings that come off another element (either rings or chains).

In traditional tatting patterns, you may know TOR's as rings that are in the middle of a chain. These rings were historically known as 'second-shuttle' elements or rings because they necessitated the use of a second shuttle to easily, effectively tat them. *ILLUS A*

In Split Ring Tatting (SRT) as in Traditional Tatting (TT) Take Off Rings increase design possibilities.

Since 2 shuttles are used in Split Ring Tatting, there is always a shuttle thread source to facilitate easy creation of Take Off Rings.

Take Off Rings can arise/be done from either portion of the split ring. But if they arise from the first/transferred double stitch portion of the split ring, the thread source to tat the Take Off Rings must come from a third shuttle/thread source and be carried along the ring thread inside the double stitches. This is known as Padded Tatting. *Use of Padded Tatting technique will be featured in Book 3 of this series, "More Fun with Split Ring Tatting".*

Take Off Rings can easily be made (without the need for an additional thread source) if they are made/tatted from the second portion of the split ring.

Note: The patterns in this book were carefully written/laid out so that if you follow the path/plan and tat the split ring portions in the order and the way they were are illustrated you can tat the patterns with only two thread sources and use of regular joins, not split ring joining technique.

In this book Take Off Rings are always associated with a split ring. The Split Ring and its associated Take Off Ring is tatted as a unit but in steps.

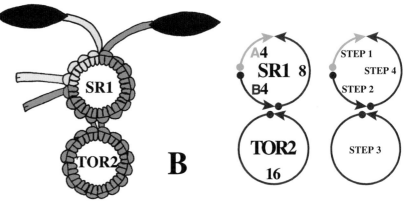

Step by Step Directions as to How to Tat Example in ILLUS B

Step 1: With Shuttle A form a ring and make 4 regular, transferred double stitches.
Step 2: With Shuttle B--Make 4 reverse, untransferred double stitches on the ring thread. Reverse work.
Step 3: With Shuttle B--tat Take Off Ring 2: Make 16 regular, transferred double stitches. Close Take Off Ring 2. Reverse work.
Step 4: With Shuttle B--make 8 reverse, untransferred double stitches on the ring thread. Close Split Ring 1 by pulling Shuttle A thread.
Steps 1, 2, & 4 create the split ring. Step 3 creates the take-off ring.

More than one TOR can be made coming from a single split ring.

ILLUS C shows a split ring (#2) with 3 Take Off Rings (#3,4,5). Rings #1 & 6 are tatted as regular rings.

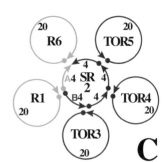

GUIDE/KEY TO SPLIT RING VISUAL PATTERNS

KEY POINTS OF ILLUSTRATED PATTERNS

Color of Portions/Segments
> -Each color represents one of two shuttle/thread sources

Direction of the arcs (from dot to arrowheads)
> -Shows which way regular rings and the portions of split rings are worked.
> -Gives direction as to how the ring is to be tatted if Frontside/Backside Tatting technique is used.
> -Gives direction as to when the work is to be reversed.

Colored Letters
> -Dictates which portion of a split ring is to be tatted first ('A') with regular, transferred double stitches and then the ('B') portion with untransferred, reverse-stitch double stitches.
> -If a split ring does not have a join or a TOR associated with it, the portions of the split ring can be tatted in any order (colored letters will not be indicated in this split ring).

Numbered Rings
> All the rings (both regular or split ring) are numbered sequentially. Thus the path that the pattern is to be worked is to start at 'R1' and work in ascending order.

There are different ways or paths to take to tat the pattern other than the one that I have illustrated. However, the patterns have been carefully designed and charted to lessen the complexity of the pattern and to allow for the following conditions:
> -The pattern can be completed in one round (or minimal numbers of rounds).
> -Regular joins (not Split Ring Joining technique) can be used.
> > -Regular joins must be made on the first portion of the split ring (the regular, transferred double stitches).
> -Take off rings (TOR's) can be created without the need for an additional thread source.
> > -TOR's are created (with only two shuttles/thread sources used) on the second portion of the split ring (the untransferred, reverse-stitch double stitches).
> > -TOR's (which are regular rings) allow regular joins to be used.
> -Regular rings are used as often as possible.

REGULARLY TATTED RINGS AS SEEN IN VISUAL PATTERNS--INCLUDING TAKE OFF RINGS

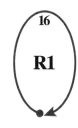

●   The <u>dot</u> is used to designate the starting point of the ring.

◢   The <u>arrowhead</u> designates the ending point of the ring.

'R' is used to designate a (regular) ring.

The larger 'number' (after the 'R') designates the order in which the rings are tatted and thus how the pattern is worked.

As in other visual/diagrammed patterns, the '#' on the inside of the arc is the number of double stitches in that particular portion of the ring and/or between picots and joins.

A regular-tatted ring in Visual Pattern style is distinguished by the fact that:
> -There is only one arc.
> -There is only one color used for the arc, starting dot and ending arrowhead.
> -The starting point and the ending point are at the same place on the ring.

SPLIT RINGS IN VISUAL PATTERNS

 Two <u>dots</u> of different colors are used to designate the starting points of the two different thread sources of a split ring. Each thread source has its own starting-point dot for every split ring.

 Two <u>arrowheads</u> are used to designate the ending points of the two thread sources of a split ring. Each thread source has it own ending-point arrowhead for every split ring.

 The <u>arcs</u> represent the different thread sources of the split ring. When you see a ring diagram with two colors in it, you know that it is a split ring.

The abbreviations '**SR**' are used. The '**S**' meaning 'Split' and the '**R**' meaning 'Ring'.

The larger '**#**' (after '**SR**') designates the order in which the rings are tatted and thus how the pattern is worked.

As in other visual/diagrammed patterns, the number on the inside of the arc is the number of double stitches in that particular portion of the split ring and/or between picots and joins.

When all the illustrations are put into one diagram, the complete path of where the split ring is started, where it ends, the direction that the portions of the split rings are made, and stitch counts of the portions of the split ring designate the attributes of the split ring.

COLORED LETTERS IN VISUAL PATTERNS

Some of the split rings in the visual patterns will have colored letter designations before the double stitch number and some will not.

If a split ring does not have a join or a Take Off Ring associated with it, the portions of the split ring can be tatted in any order.

ILLUS A is a split ring that can be tatted in one of two ways--either choice appropriate:
   A. The 12-stitch (red) portion can be tatted first with regular, transferred stitches and then the 4-stitch (green) portion is tatted with reverse, untransferred stitches. **OR**
   B. Tat the 4-stitch (green) portion first with regular, transferred stitches and then the 12-stitch (red) portion is tatted with reverse, untransferred stitches.

However, the order in which the split ring portions are tatted in some split rings is important for two reasons:
   1. To easily create ***joins*** utilizing traditional tatting joining techinque--NOT split ring joining tatting (which is more cumbersome to master and doesn't create as visually-effective a join).
      --Done from the ***first portion*** (the regular, transferred double stitches) of the split ring.
   2. To effect the creation of ***Take-Off Rings (TOR's)*** without the need to use a third thread source.
      --Done from the ***second portion*** (the reverse, untransferred double stitches) of the split ring.

The presence of colored letters in ***ILLUS B*** dictates that the 12-stitch (red) portion is to be tatted first with regular, transferred stitches and then the 4-stitch (green) portion is tatted second with reverse, untransferred stitches.   Just like in the alphabet, 'A' comes before 'B' and thus the 'A' portion is done first.

NUMBERED RINGS IN VISUAL PATTERNS

How the pattern is worked (or the 'Path' of how the pattern is worked) is designated in Visual Patterns by the number inside the rings, next to either **R**, **SR**, or **TOR**.

Start at R1 and then progress numerically (1 then 2, then 3, then 4.....) through the pattern.

DIRECTION OF ARCS

The direction in which the arc is illustrated will give you clues as to:
>   A. If the ring/split ring is to be tatted as a 'Frontside' or a 'Backside' element.
>   B. When you need to Reverse or Turn the Work (traditional written directions use 'RW' or 'T').

C

CLOCKWISE
Direction of Work
'Frontside' Ring
DS = Under then
Over Stitch

VISUAL PATTERN CLUES AS TO USE OF FRONTSIDE/BACKSIDE TATTING
(See later information on Frontside/Backside Tatting, pages 21 through 24)

The direction of the arc (as evidenced by the arrowhead) shows the direction that the ring is worked.

Traditionally tatted regular rings are tatted in a 'clockwise' direction.

If the arc of a regular ring is *'clockwise'* then the ring is tatted as a *'frontside'* ring.   **ILLUS C**

If the arc of a regular ring is *'counter-clockwise'* then the ring is tatted as a *'backside'* ring. **ILLUS D**

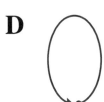

D

COUNTER-CLOCKWISE
Direction of Work
'Backside' Ring
DS = Over then
Under Stitch

However, in split rings, both clockwise and counter-clockwise arcs/portions are part of each split ring. The direction of the first portion of the split ring made dictates whether the split ring is tatted as either a 'frontside' or a 'backside' ring.

ILLUS E is a 'Frontside' split ring because Portion A is 'clockwise'.

ILLUS D is a 'Backside' split ring because Portion A is 'counter-clockwise'.

E

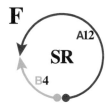

CLOCKWISE First
= 'Frontside' Ring

With the 'Red' Shuttle make 12 regular, transferred double stitches: *Under stitch-first; followed by Over Stitch.*
With 'Green' Shuttle make 4 reverse, untranferred double stitches: *Over Stitch-First; followed by Under Stitch.*

F

COUNTER-CLOCKWISE
First = 'Backside' Ring

With the 'Red' Shuttle make 12 regular, transferred double stitches: *Over Stitch-first; followed by Under Stitch.*
With 'Green' Shuttle make 4 reverse, untranferred double stitches: *Under Stitch-First; followed by Over Stitch.*

If the split ring is not designated as to which portion is made first, it is up to the tatter to decide which portion to work first then second and thus, whether the split ring is either a 'frontside' or a 'backside' ring.

VISUAL PATTERN CLUES AS TO WHEN TO REVERSE WORK

If you tat one ring as a 'frontside' element (the first portion of a split ring &/or the regular ring is a clock-wise arc) and then the second ring is a 'backside' element (the first portion of a split ring &/or the regular ring is a counter-clockwise arrow) you will need to Reverse Work between these two rings.   *ILLUS G*

G

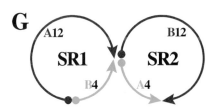

STEP BY STEP INSTRUCTIONS AS TO HOW TO READ VISUAL PATTERNS--EXAMPLE A

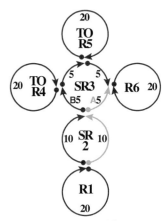

Ring 1 is a regularly-tatted ring. Only one shuttle/thread source is needed. Tat 20 regular, transferred double stitches and close the ring.

The next ring is Split Ring 2. It is an example of an 'even' split ring. To tat this ring you will need a second shuttle/thread source. Since no colored letters are used in this illustration, either portion (the green or the red shuttle/thread source) can be tatted first/second. One way to create this Split Ring is to use the red shuttle/thread source to tat 10 regular, transferred double stitches. Then use the green shuttle/thread source to tat 10 reverse, untransferred double stitches. Close the ring by pulling the red shuttle/thread source.

Ring #3 is an uneven Split Ring with two Take-Off Rings associated with it (TOR4 & TOR5). These three rings (SR3, TOR4 & TOR5) are tatted as a unit in 6 steps:

Step 1: With the green shuttle/thread source tat 5 regular, transferred double stitches. You know to use this shuttle/thread source because of the colored-letter 'A' associated with this portion of the split ring.

Step 2: With the red shuttle/thread source tat 5 reverse, untransferred double stitches.

Step 3: Take Split Ring 3 off your hand. Reverse work. With the red shuttle/thread tat Take Off Ring 4 as a regular ly-tatted ring of 20 transferred double stitches. Close Take Off Ring 4. Reverse work.

Step 4: Put Split Ring 3 back onto your hand. With the red shuttle/thread source tat 5 more reverse, untransferred, double stitches.

Step 5: Take Split Ring 3 off your hand. Reverse work. With the red shuttle/thread tat Take Off Ring 5 as a regular ly-tatted ring of 20 transferred double stitches. Close Take Off Ring 5. Reverse work.

Step 6: Put Split Ring 3 back onto your hand. With the red shuttle/thread source tat 5 more reverse, untransferred double stitches. Close Split Ring 3 by pulling the green shuttle/thread source.

Ring 6 is a regularly-tatted ring. Only one shuttle/thread source is needed. Either thread source can be used. Tat 20 regular, transferred double stitches and then close the ring.

Notes on directions of the arrows of the rings and their various portions and relationship to Frontside/Backside Tatting Technique:
 --R1 = the red arc is clockwise--this is a 'frontside' ring.
 --SR2--depends upon which shuttle/thread source is used first. If the red shuttle/thread is used for the first step of the split ring then the arc is clockwise thus it is a 'frontside' ring. Both portions are tatted the same way--as frontside' stitches. However, if the green shuttle/thread source is used first, the arc of this portion is counter-clockwise. Thus the entire split ring would be tatted as a 'backside' ring.
 --SR3 directs you to tat the green shuttle/thread source first and since this arc is counter-clockwise the entire Split Ring 3 would be tatted as a 'backside' ring.
 --TOR4, TOR5 & R5 are all clockwise and thus are 'frontside' rings using the red shuttle/thread source.
 --Because SR3 is a 'backside' ring and then TOR4 is a 'frontside' ring, you will need to Reverse Work when going from SR3/to TOR4 These same steps are true when going to/from SR3 and TOR5. Another Reverse Work is needed when going from SR3 (a 'backside' ring) to R6 (a 'frontside' ring).

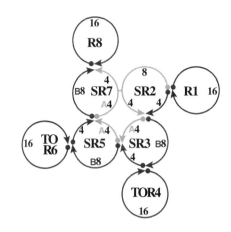

Ring 1 is a regularly-tatted ring. Only one shuttle/thread source is needed. Tat 16 transferred double stitches and then close the ring.

The next ring is Split Ring 2. It is an example of an 'uneven' split ring. To tat this ring you will need a second shuttle/thread source. Since no colored letters are used in this illustration, either portion (the green or the red shuttle/thread source) can be tatted first/second. One way to create this Split Ring is to use the green shuttle/thread source to tat 8 regular, transferred double stitches, a joining picot, and then 4 more regular, transferred double stitches. Then use the red shuttle/thread source to tat 4 reverse, untransferred double stitches. Close the ring by pulling the green shuttle/thread source.

Split Ring 3 has Take Off Ring 4 (TOR4) associated with it. These two rings (SR3 & TOR4) are tatted as a unit in 4 steps:

> Step 1: With the green shuttle/thread source tat 4 regular, transferred double stitches. You know to use this shuttle/thread source because of the colored-letter 'A' associated with this portion of the split ring.

> Step 2: With the red shuttle/thread source tat 8 reverse, untransferred double stitches. This portion is designated 'B'.

> Step 3: Take Split Ring 3 off your hand. Reverse work. With the red shuttle/thread tat Take Off Ring 4 as a regular ly-tatted ring of 16 transferred double stitches. Close Take Off Ring 4. Reverse work.

> Step 4: Put Split Ring 3 back onto your hand. With the red shuttle/thread source tat 4 more reverse, untransferred double stitches. Close Split Ring 3 by pulling the green shuttle/thread source.

Split Ring 5 and Take Off Ring 6 are tatted as a unit the same way as Split Ring 3 and Take Off Ring 4.

Split Ring 7 has a join to Split Ring 2 and thus the pattern directs you to use the green shuttle/thread source first ('A') to tat 4 regular, transferred double stitches, join to the picot of Split Ring 2, followed by 4 regular, transferred double stitches. Then with the red shuttle/thread source ('B') tat 8 reverse, untransferred double stitches. Close Split Ring 7 by pulling the green shuttle/thread source.

Ring 8 is a regularly-tatted ring. Only one shuttle/thread source is needed. Either thread source can be used. Tat 16 regular, transferred double stitches and then close the ring.

Notes on directions of the arrows of the rings and their various portions and its relationship to Frontside/Backside Tatting Technique:
> *--R1: Arc is clockwise--tatted as a 'frontside' ring.*
> *--SR2: depends upon which shuttle thread you use first. If green shuttle/thread is used first it will be a 'backside split ring. If the red shuttle/thread is used first, the split ring will be 'frontside'.*
> *--SR3, SR5 and SR7: The green shuttle/thread is directed to be used first and thus these split rings are 'backside' elements.*
> *--TOR 4, TOR 6 and R8 are all 'frontside' rings.*

This motif is featured in __Fun With Split Ring Tatting: Book 2__ and is called the "Houndstooth Motif".

SPECIAL CONSTRUCTION & ENHANCEMENT TECHNIQUES

ALL RINGS ARE TATTED WITH NO-SPACE OF THREAD BETWEEN RINGS

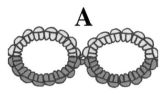

The visual effect of the pieces in this book is that each ring is closely adjacent to its neighboring ring(s). **ILLUS A**

In the same way that Joining Picots are used to simulate no space of thread between rings, all rings are started as close to one another as possible.

The challenge is to tat a piece so that an observer is unaware of the path of construction of the piece.

PICOT SIZE--USE OF JOINING PICOTS

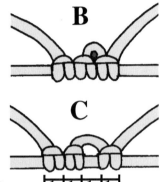

The picots used in this book are all examples of Joining Picots.   The pieces were designed with the idea that all the rings lie in close relationship with one another.

Joining picots are minute picots that barely allow for insertion of a tiny crochet hook. They are used only for joining, not as ornamental picots. A Joining Picot is barely recognizable as a picot loop. **ILLUS B**

A proper Joining Picot size is equal to one double stitch width. **ILLUS C**

A space of thread between the two double stitches that is creating the picot is equal to one double stitch width.

JOINING TOOLS

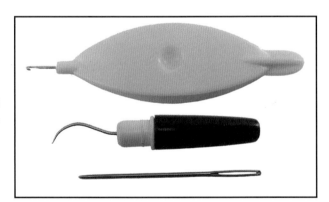

In the process of facilitating very tight joins between rings, very small joining picots are created. A small-gauge crochet hook is necessary to facilitate these joins.
   Crochet hook range: Size 8 to 14. *(14 is the smallest).*

Proper Joining Picot size is actually so small that at times it maybe dificult to get even a tiny crochet hook into the picot loop to use it. At these times, a dental-pick tool or a blunt-tipped sewing needle (such as a Tapestry needle--ca. Size 20, 22, or 24--*larger # equals smaller needle*) is handy to use to pull the picots out to a sufficient size to be able to easily insert a hook to use as a join.

Author's Favorite Split Ring Tatting Tools

FORGOTTEN JOINING PICOT?

Not all hope is lost! Just insert your crochet hook or pick/needle between the stitches where the picot should be. Pull out this horizontal space of thread and use it as a picot. Picots formed this way will be an appropriate size for joining the patterns tatted with Split Ring Tatting technique in this book.

You can also add on to a previously-made piece, making it longer/larger by pulling out joining picots between stitches.

USE OF AN EXTRA HALF STITCH ON FIRST PORTION OF SPLIT RINGS AND REGUALR RINGS

There is a subtle difference in how the double stitches stack up and the space they occupy in the first portion (the regular, transferred double stitch side) versus the second portion (the reverse, untransferred double stitch side) of the split ring.

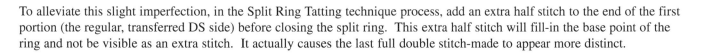

The act of closing the ring causes the last half stitch of the first portion (the regular, transferred DS side) to be compressed into the ending point or base of the ring/split ring.

This effect becomes apparent if you tat several Even Split Rings. *Even split rings are those made with the same number of double stitches on each portion of the split ring (eg. SR: 8 / 8).* The second portion will be slightly bigger. This may not be grossly apparent with just one ring...but with a row of rings, the piece will show a slight curving effect.

To alleviate this slight imperfection, in the Split Ring Tatting technique process, add an extra half stitch to the end of the first portion (the regular, transferred DS side) before closing the split ring. This extra half stitch will fill-in the base point of the ring and not be visible as an extra stitch. It actually causes the last full double stitch-made to appear more distinct.

The author also adds the extra half stitch to all of her regularly-tatted rings, including Take Off Rings, with no detrimental effect to the piece's overall finished appearance nor to the structural integrity.

DROPPING THE SHUTTLE THROUGH THE RING BEFORE CLOSING THE RING ON 'FRONTSIDE' RING ELEMENTS

Just before closing a frontside-tatted ring (either a regular or a split ring), drop the shuttle through the ring from top to bottom. Then close the ring as normal.

This will push the last double stitch made up at the base of the closed ring, allowing the last double stitch to appear more like all the other stitches.

If you are closing a backside-tatted ring, do **not** drop the shuttle through the ring before closing it. Just close a backside-tatted ring as is traditional/normal.

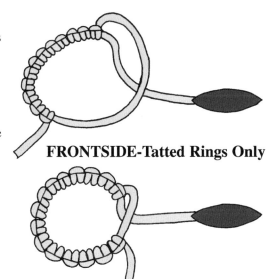

FRONTSIDE-Tatted Rings Only

CLOSING RINGS TO ACHIEVE A SPECIFIC SHAPE: TEARDROP VS ROUND SHAPE

The shape of a traditionally-closed ring is 'teardrop' shaped, somewhat pointed at the base of the ring where the first and last double stitches come together. Traditional tatting pattern designers have historically recognized and have created patterns with that shape in mind.

To achieve this shape, the ring is closed by pulling the working shuttle/thread downward, away from the base of the ring   *ILLUS A*

However, all the rings in this book are designed to be ROUND-shaped.

One may be tempted to close a ring by pulling the shuttle/thread toward the side of the ring while closing the ring. *ILLUS B*   This will erroneously produce a misshapen ring due to the fact that the last double stitch-made will not align with the first double stitch-made. ***Black Arrow in ILLUS B***

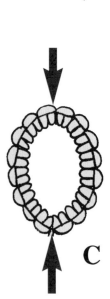

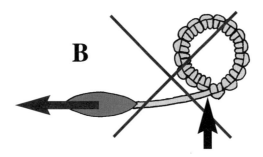

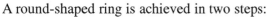

A round-shaped ring is achieved in two steps:
    1. Close the ring as in ILLUS A by pulling the working shuttle/thread downward, away from the base of the ring.
    2. Use your fingers to push the ring into a round shape by pushing the ring in the direction of the arrows in ILLUS C.

NEATENING THE RINGS AND STITCHES

After closing each ring:

    --Use your fingers to push the ring into a round shape.

    --Use your fingernails to push the picots in the joins into place as close as possible to the new ring's horizontal thread region.

    --Use your fingernails to push the double stitches at the base of the ring down to be in the same plane as the rest of the double stitches.

    --Pull on picots to neaten the double stitches on either side of the picot. You can also use your fingernails to push down the double stitchs on either side of the picot so that they lie in the same planes as the other stitches of the ring.
        --In the creation of a picot, the picot loop is actually the horizontal space of thread on the backside of the work between double stitches. When this horizontal thread is elongated into a picot loop, the stitches on either side of the picot are put at a slight instability.

USE OF FRONTSIDE/BACKSIDE TATTING & JOINING TECHNIQUE STRATEGIES

**Frontside/Backside Tatting Technique** is the formation of the Half/Double Stitches, Elements (Rings and Chains), and Joins in such a way that the 'reversed elements' would have the same appearance as the 'unreversed elements'. One side of the piece would have a 'frontside' appearance and the other side of the piece a 'backside' appearance. This has also been known as 'Directional Tatting'. The name of 'Rightside/Wrongside Tatting' should not be used...there is a fair amount of aversion to this name by the tatting community. It is thought that there is no 'wrong' side to tatted lace.

Disclaimer: Frontside/Backside Tatting Technique is a tatting 'strategy'. It is not a required technique, but is an optional approach. Use or no use of Frontside/Backside Tatting is a personal choice. It does add a level of complexity to the tatting process. It is a challenge that you may choose to use at certain times. Example: you may choose the challenge when tatting a basic tatting pattern that you have done many times and even almost know by heart. Use of FS/BS Tatting may give you that little extra brain challenge that you are missing. However, in more advanced patterns (example: two-colored work) the use of FS/BS Tatting becomes more beneficial and thus less of a choice. There is nothing that can alienate a friendly group of tatters quicker than the mention of Frontside/Backside Tatting techniques. There are some tatters that believe that FS/BS Tatting is the only way to tat. Those who choose not to tat this way, take it as a personal attack that their work is inferior. This author has had someone approach her after introducing the concept of FS/BS Tatting in a class/workshop situation. This tatter said quite bluntly that she "had never had a piece of her tatting returned to her after giving it as a gift because it was NOT tatted with FS/BS technique!". I was stunned by this remark and since then have learned to be very careful about how I presented the concept of FS/BS Tatting technique. I never say it is a required technique--that it is instead a personal/optional choice.

There are two areas of tatting that will show if Frontside/Backside Tatting Technique has been used:
1. The double stitch formation process - most visible at the picots.
2. Joins.

Frontside/Backside Tatting in regard to the Double Stitches

First we need to define and understand the double stitch formation process.

The double stitch is formed of two half stitches that are titled: 'Over Stitch' and 'Under Stitch'. These two half stitches are in effect mirror images/opposites of each other.

Under Stitch--made by passing the working shuttle first _**under**_, around, then over the ring thread followed by transferring the loop from the working shuttle thread to the working thread source. _**ILLUS C**_

Over Stitch--made by passing the working shuttle first _**over**_, around, then under the ring thread followed by transferring the loop from the working shuttle thread to the working thread source. _**ILLUS D**_

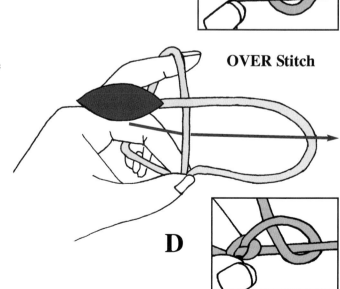

UNDER Stitch

C

OVER Stitch

D

FRONTSIDE/BACKSIDE TATTING BASICS

A double stitch formed traditionally (Under Stitch-first/Over Stitch-second) will produce what is called a 'frontside' double stitch/element. The horizontal space of thread that spans the two half stitches (*) is visible on the 'frontside' of the tatting. It is this horizontal span of thread that we count as a double stitch. ***ILLUS A/B***

The reverse side of this stitch formation process (if you turn the work over) will have the 'backside' appearance. The distinctive horizontal thread bar that we associate with a double stitch is not visible on the individual double stitch. ***ILLUS D/E***

If the order of the half stitches is reversed in creating the double stitches---Over Stitch - done first / Under Stitch - done second---the effect produced is a 'backside' double stitch. ***ILLUS D/E***

The reverse side of this stitch formation process will have the 'frontside' appearance. ***ILLUS A/B***

The effect of the order in which the half stitches are tatted to create double stitches can best be seen at the picots:

--The frontside of the double stitches at the picots will have an even appearance with no visible difference seen in the double stitches on either side of the picot. ***ILLUS C***

--On the backside of the double stitches, there will be a space where the picot is that there is no horizontal space of thread between the double stitches. The picot would have been the horizontal area of thread. ***ILLUS F***

FRONTSIDE TATTING

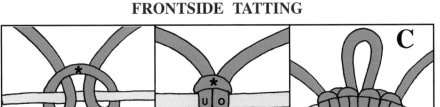

Frontside view of a Frontside DS
or
Backside View of a Backside DS

BACKSIDE TATTING

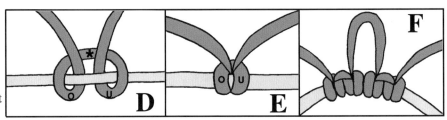

Frontside view of a Backside DS
or
Backside View of a Frontside DS

FRONTSIDE/BACKSIDE TECHNIQUE APPLIED TO SPLIT RING TATTING

As explained before, the double stitches of the second portion of the split ring are 'reverse' of the double stitches of the first portion of the split ring. Thus the order in which the half stitches are used (either Over or Under) is different between the two portions.

When a 'Backside Split Ring' is made, the order of the half stitches used on BOTH portions must be altered, in effect 'reversed'.

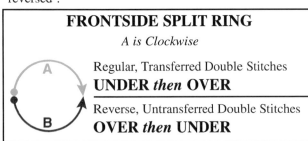

FRONTSIDE SPLIT RING

A is Clockwise

Regular, Transferred Double Stitches
UNDER *then* OVER

Reverse, Untransferred Double Stitches
OVER *then* UNDER

BACKSIDE SPLIT RING

A is Counter-Clockwise

Reverse, Untransferred Double Stitches
UNDER *then* OVER

Regular, Transferred Double Stitches
OVER *then* UNDER

Frontside/Backside Tatting in regard to Joins

The second area in which Frontside/Backside Tatting technique is visually apparent is at tatted joins.

The appropriate joining technique to use for Directional Tatting is dependent upon several factors:
1. Whether you are tatting a 'frontside' or a 'backside' element.
2. Whether or not you are joining two different colored elements in the process.

The act of making a regular (sliding, not locking) join adds an extra horizontal thread to the stitches being tatted. This horizontal thread is supplied by the picot you are joining to. This horizontal thread is the part of the join that must be managed in the tatting process to not be visually distracting.

There are two joining techniques:
1. The Traditional Join (also known as an **Up Join**)
2. A newer way to join is known as a **Down Join**.

Both techniques join two elements together. How and when they are used can produce different visual effects due to where the extra horizontal thread ends up--either on the front or backside of the elements.

Up Join

Lay the picot on top of the thread of the element you are joining together. The working thread is brought **UP** and through the picot, the shuttle passed through the loop of thread formed, and the join nestled down into position. *ILLUS E*

The horizontal thread supplied by the picot is on the ***backside*** of the work.

This join method is sometimes called a 'Frontside Join' because the horizontal space of thread is toward the 'backside' of the piece/element and does not distract from the 'frontside' of the work. In other words, the 'frontside' is visually preserved.

E

Down Join

Lay the picot below the working thread of the element you are joining together. The thread is brought **DOWN** and through the picot, the shuttle passed through the loop of thread formed, and the join nestled down into position. *ILLUS F*

The horizontal thread supplied by the picot is on the ***frontside*** of the work.

F

Variables that Dictate Which Join (Up or Down) to Use

--Current theory contends that the horizontal space of thread on the frontside, when finished with an Over Stitch, most closely matches the appearance of a regular double stitch.

--Frontside versus backside tatting:

To match in appearance, frontside elements are joined with an Up Join while backside elements are joined with a Down Join. The Up Join is opposite of a Down Join. Because the element is reversed to being worked as a backside element, the joining technique is also reversed.

--Joining different colored elements.

The horizontal space of thread can be a distraction when joining an element of one color to a picot of another color. Thus when joining two different-colored elements, a different approach is used compared to one-color tatting.

Traditional Approach to Joining Technique

When Tatting An Element As	&	Elements Being Joined Together Are	Use	Follow the Join with an
Frontside		One Color	Down Join	Over Half Stitch
Backside		One Color	Up Join	Under Half Stitch
Frontside		Two Colors	Up Join	Over Half Stitch
Backside		Two Colors	Down Join	Under Half Stitch

Modified Approach to Joining Technique

This author has a different approach to joins. She contends that the horizontal space of thread is hard to smooth down. Thus, she uses a joining technique to always place the horizontal bar of picot thread to the backside of the work.

When Tatting An Element As	&	Elements Being Joined Together Are	Use	Follow the Join with an
Frontside		One Color or Two Colors	Up Join	Over Half Stitch
Backside		One Color or Two Colors	Down Join	Under Half Stitch

1 2

Frontside View
No joins are visible

Backside View
Rnd 1, red joining picot is visible on Rnd 2, blue work *(arrows)*

PATH OF THE PATTERN

How the pattern is worked (or the 'Path' of how the pattern is worked) is designated in Visual Patterns by the number inside the rings, next to either **R**, **SR**, or **TOR**.

Start at R1 and then progress numerically (1 then 2, then 3, then 4.....) through the pattern.

The author/designer has very carefully charted the paths through the patterns so that:
   --The pattern can be worked continuously, from start to end in one round (or as few rounds as possible).
   --Joins can be made as regular joins (not Split Ring Tatting Joins).
   --Take Off Rings can be created.

BOOKMARK VERSUS EDGING PATTERN

Many of the patterns in this book can be used to create either a bookmark (ca. 5-6 inches long) or edgings of unknown length.

As much of the pattern was included in this book that would allow a full-size pattern to be printed on a page. Thus the patterns look like 'bookmarks'.

Directions for using the pattern as an edging are included in the boxes.

Each box will have 3 lines of text/directions.

EXAMPLE:

R1 thru SR2
SR3 thru SR8
SR27 thru R34

Line 1 will be the pattern directions to START the edging.

Line 2 will be the REPEAT components of the pattern.
Repeat these directions to achieve the length of edging you desire.

Line 3 will be directions to COMPLETE/END the edging pattern.

KEY TO VISUAL PATTERNS
See Pages 13 through 15

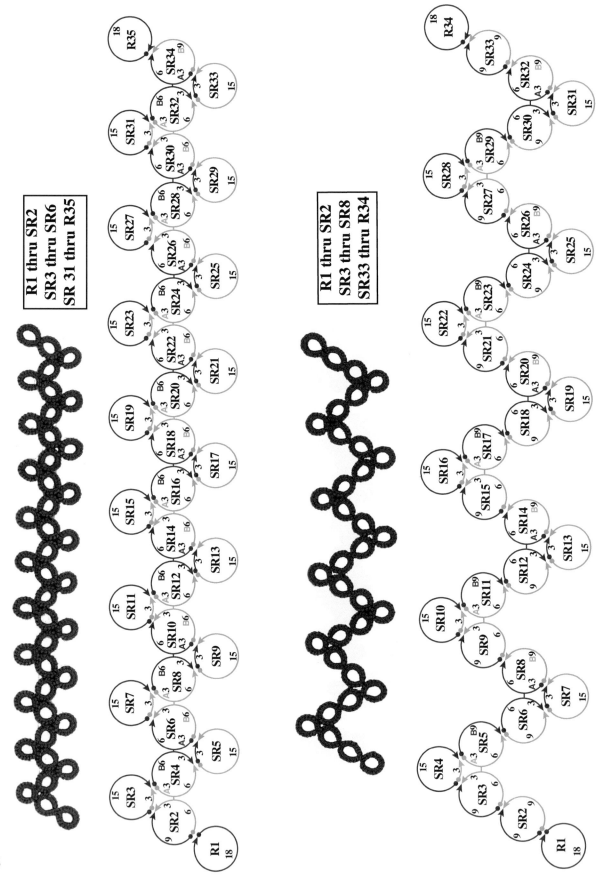

**R1 thru SR2
SR3 thru SR6
SR 31 thru R35**

**R1 thru SR2
SR3 thru SR8
SR33 thru R34**

26

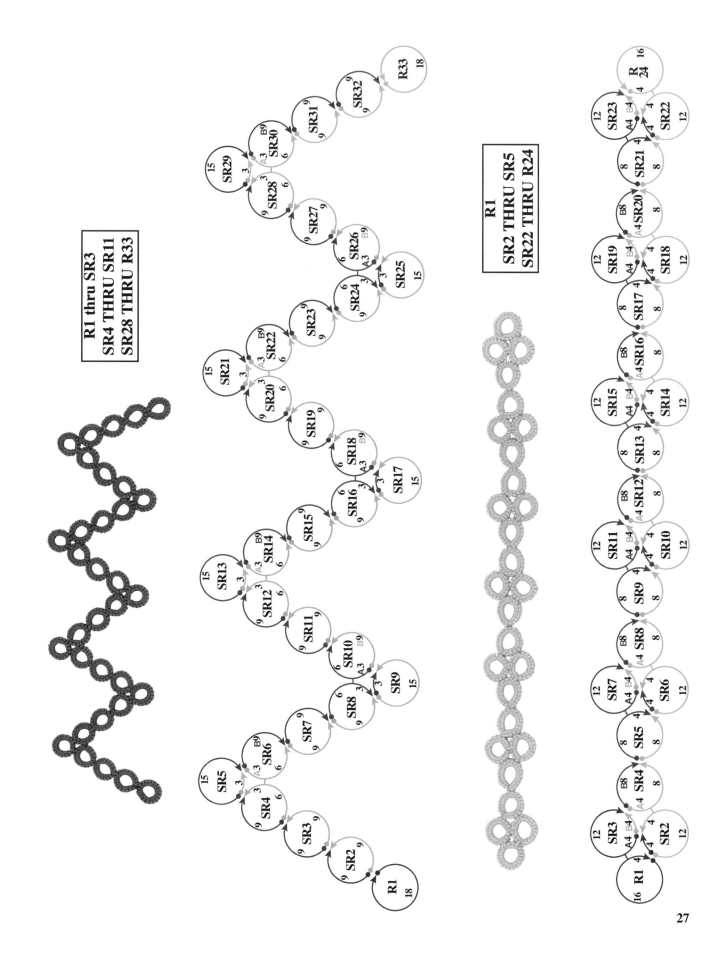

R1 thru SR3
SR4 THRU SR11
SR28 THRU R33

R1
SR2 THRU SR5
SR22 THRU R24

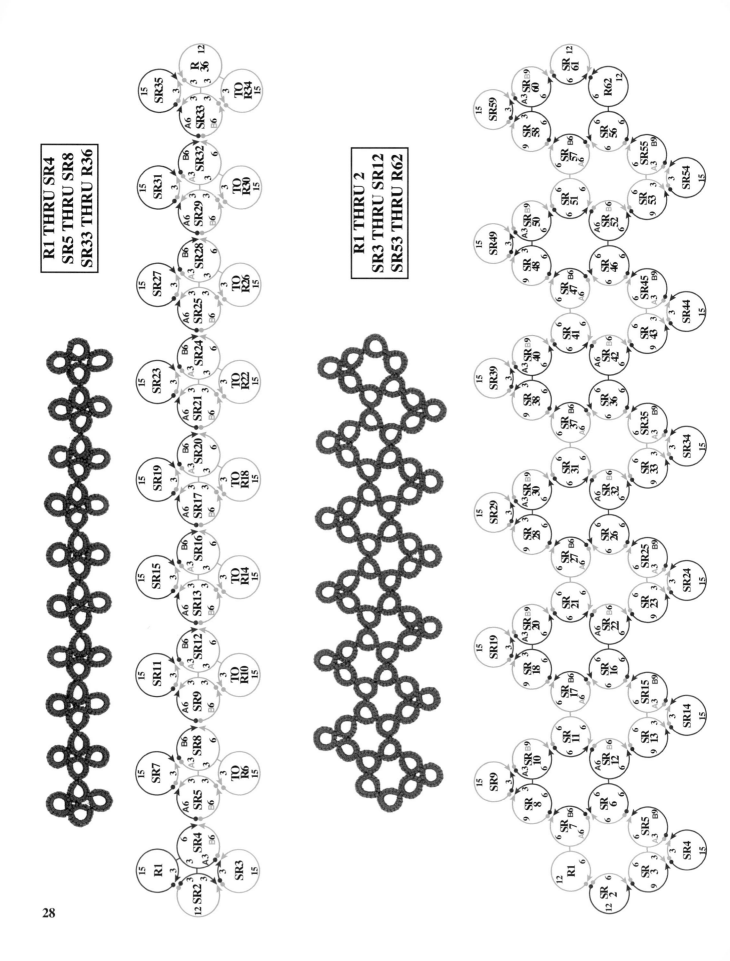

R1 THRU SR4
SR5 THRU SR8
SR33 THRU R36

R1 THRU 2
SR3 THRU SR12
SR53 THRU R62

28

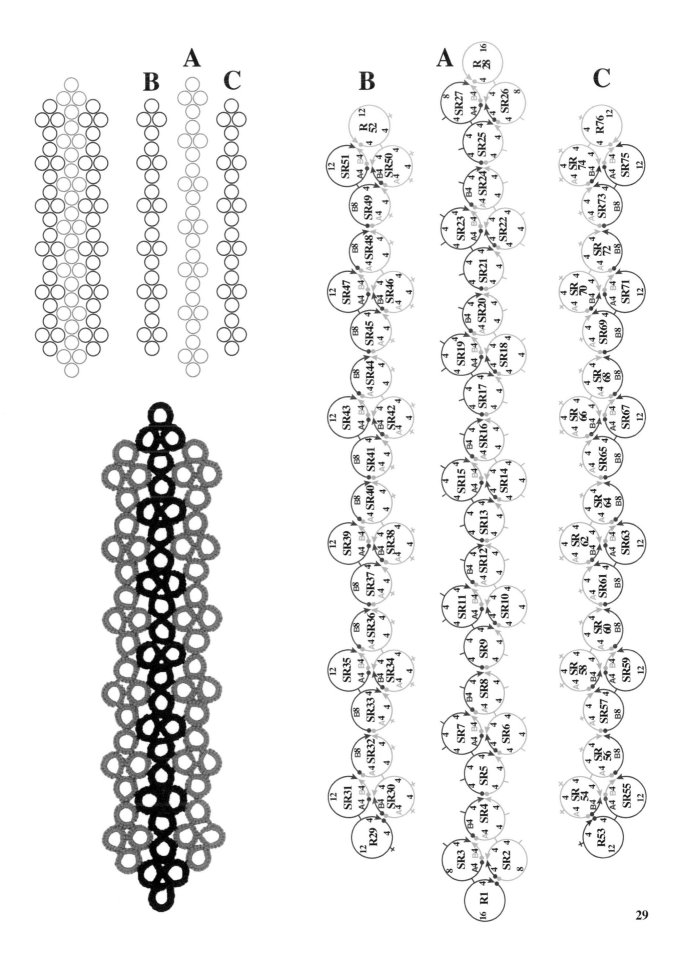

29

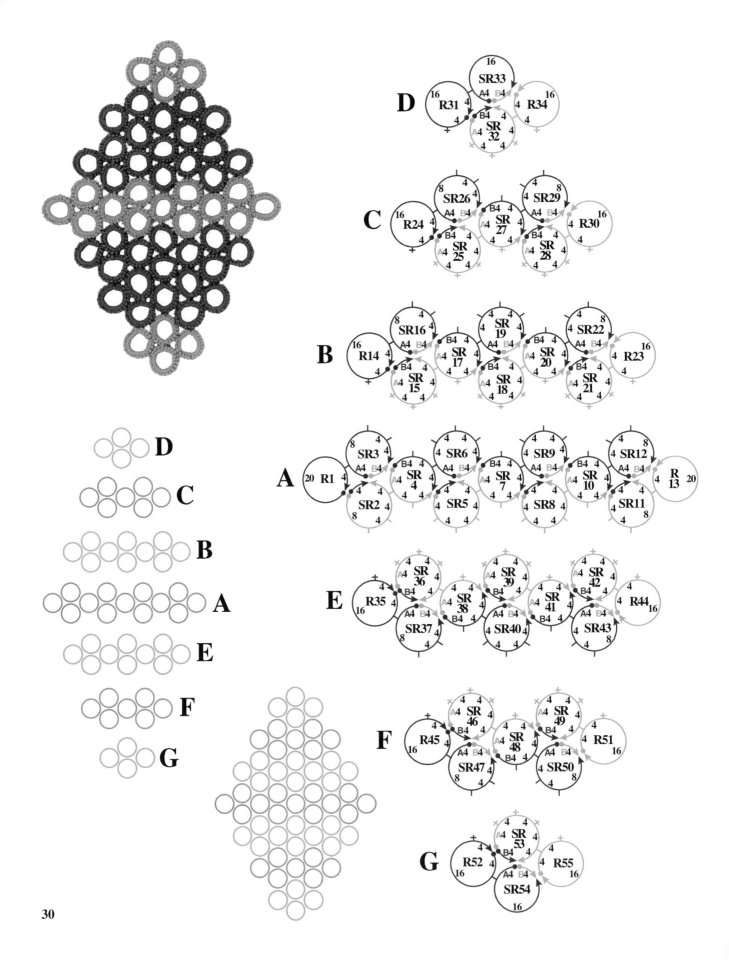

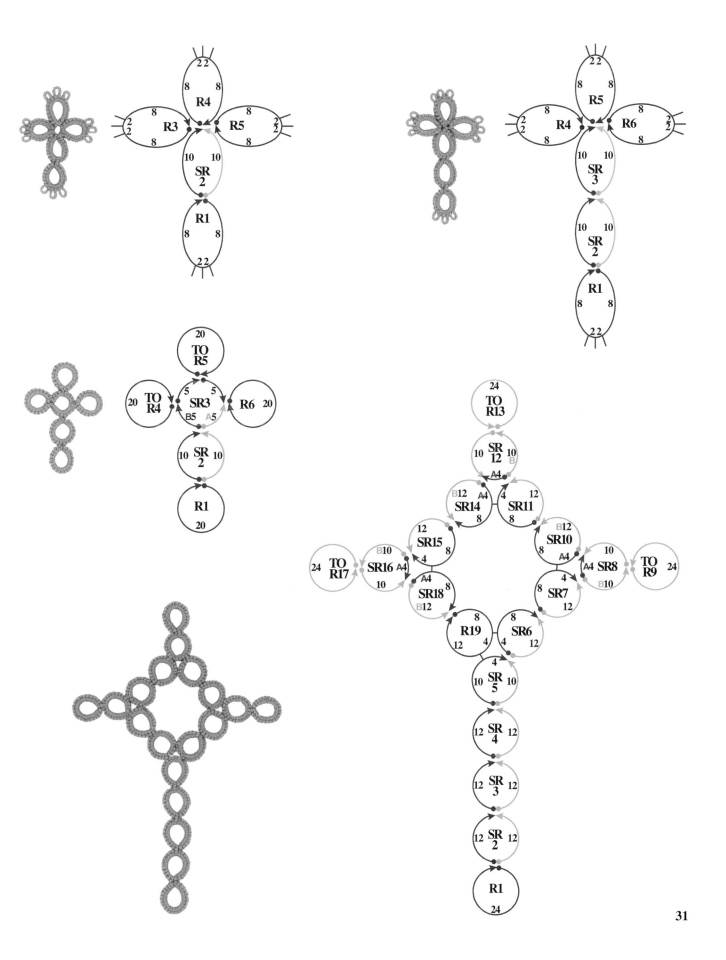

Two-Color Motif

32

Two-Color Motif

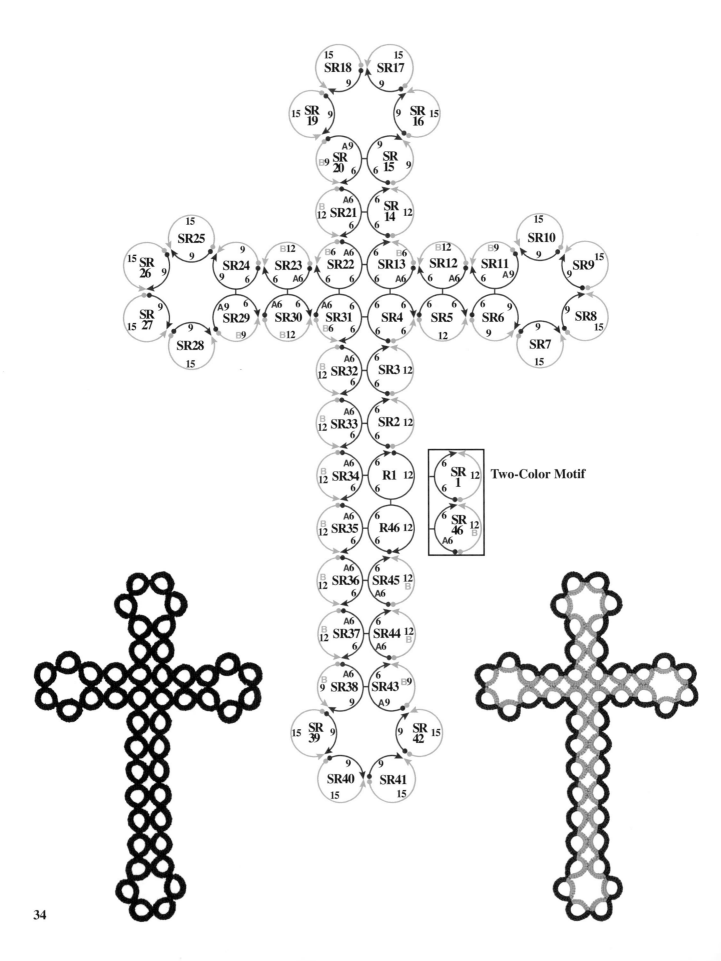

Two-Color Motif

34

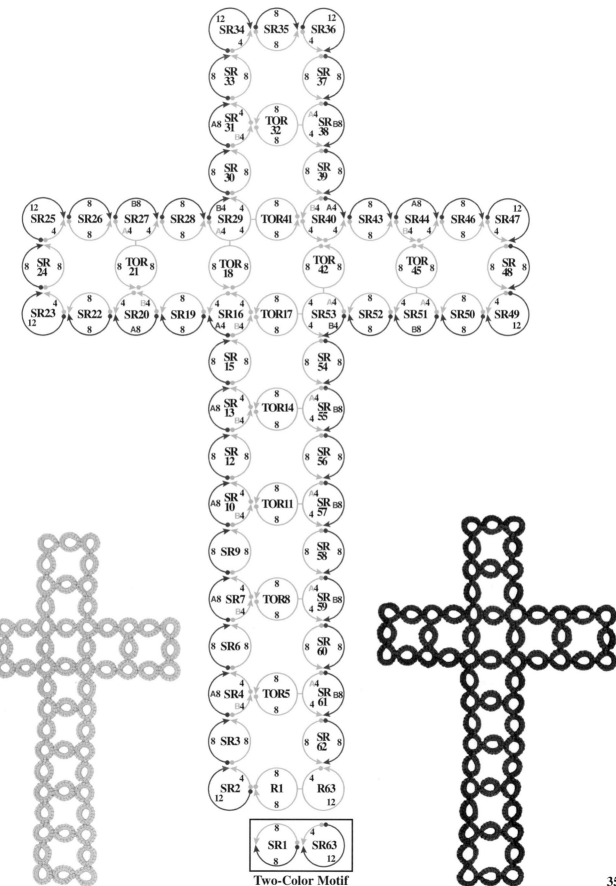

Two-Color Motif

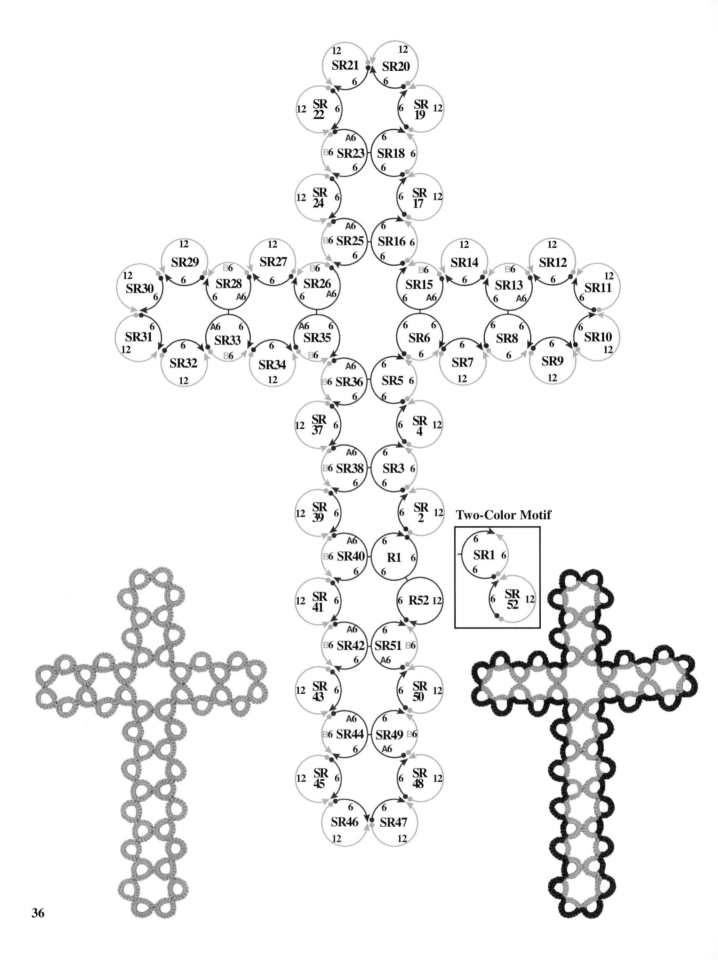

Two-Color Motif

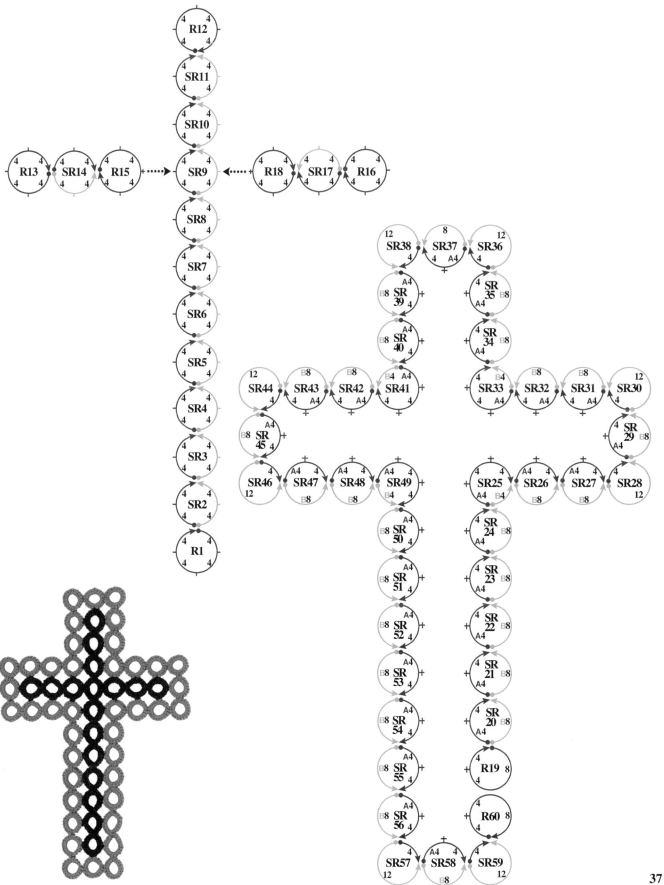

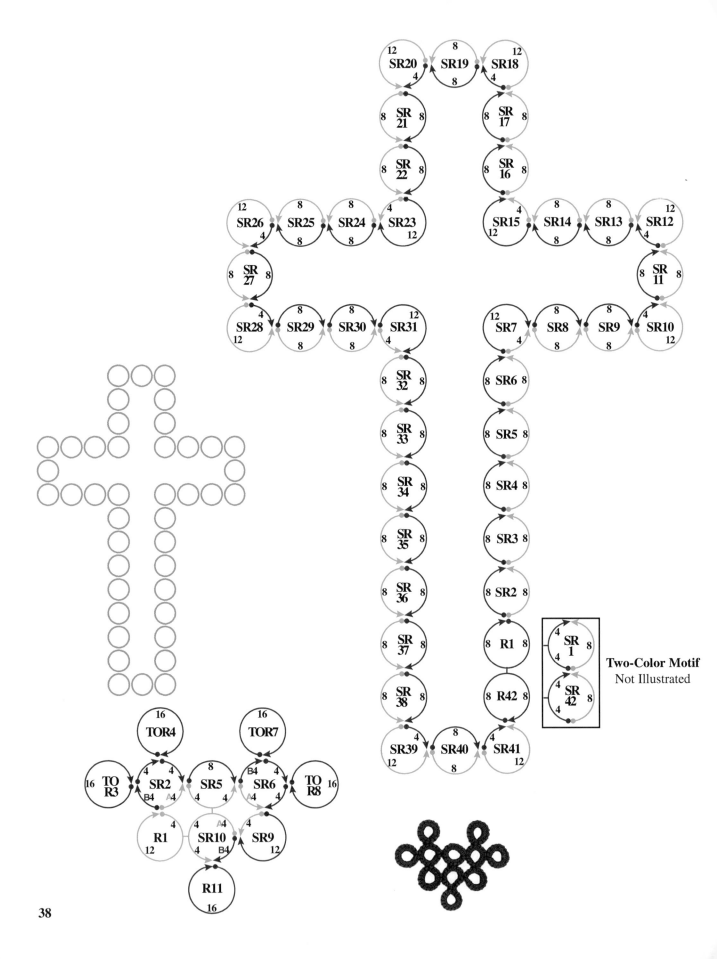

Two-Color Motif
Not Illustrated

38

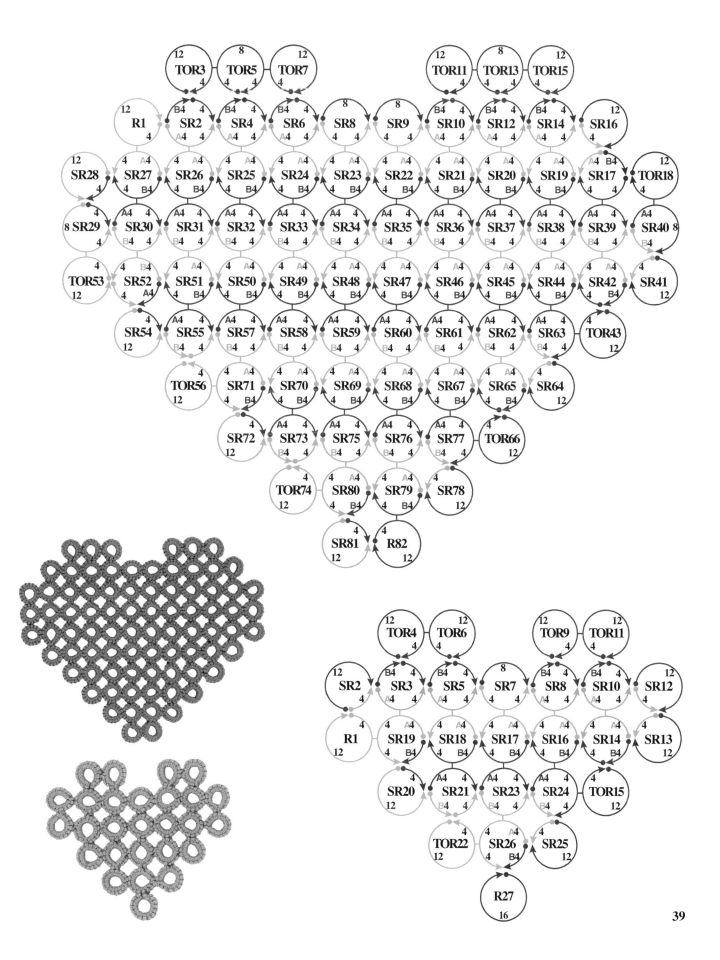

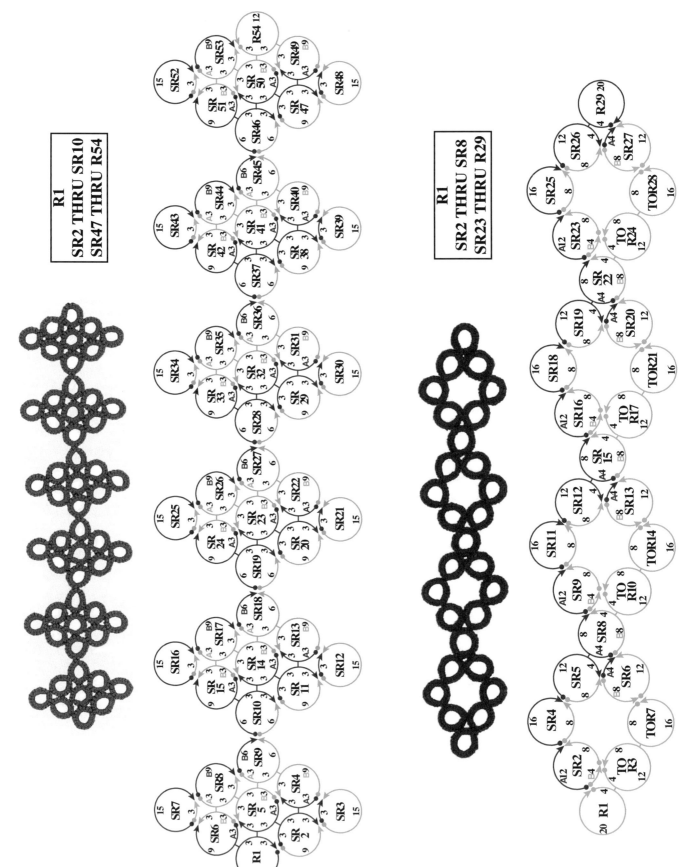

R1
SR2 THRU SR10
SR47 THRU R54

R1
SR2 THRU SR8
SR23 THRU R29

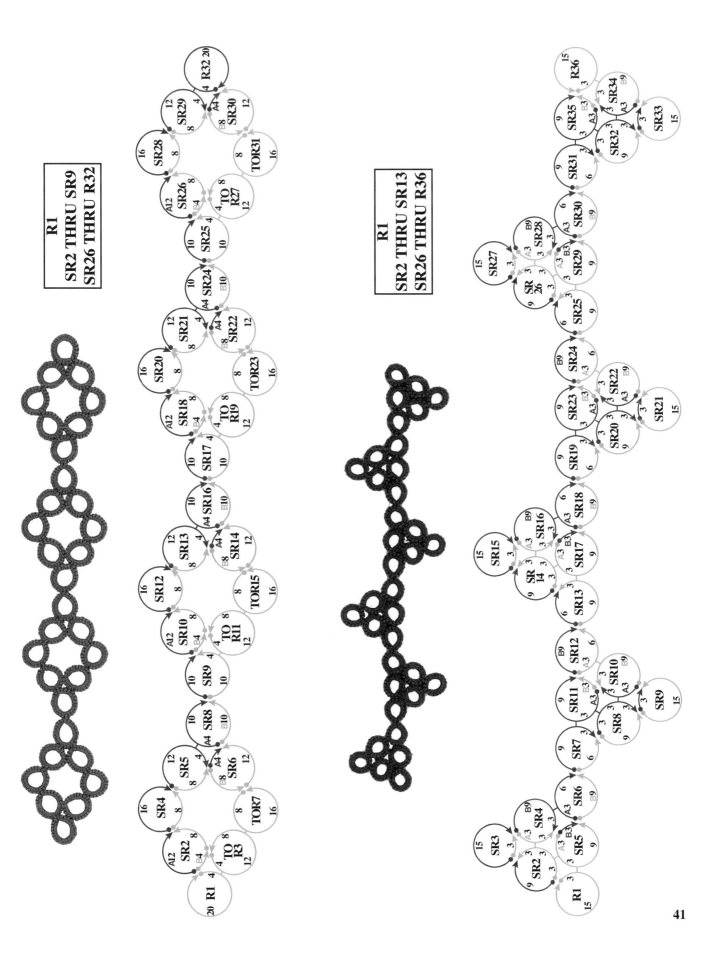

R1
SR2 THRU SR9
SR26 THRU R32

R1
SR2 THRU SR13
SR26 THRU R36

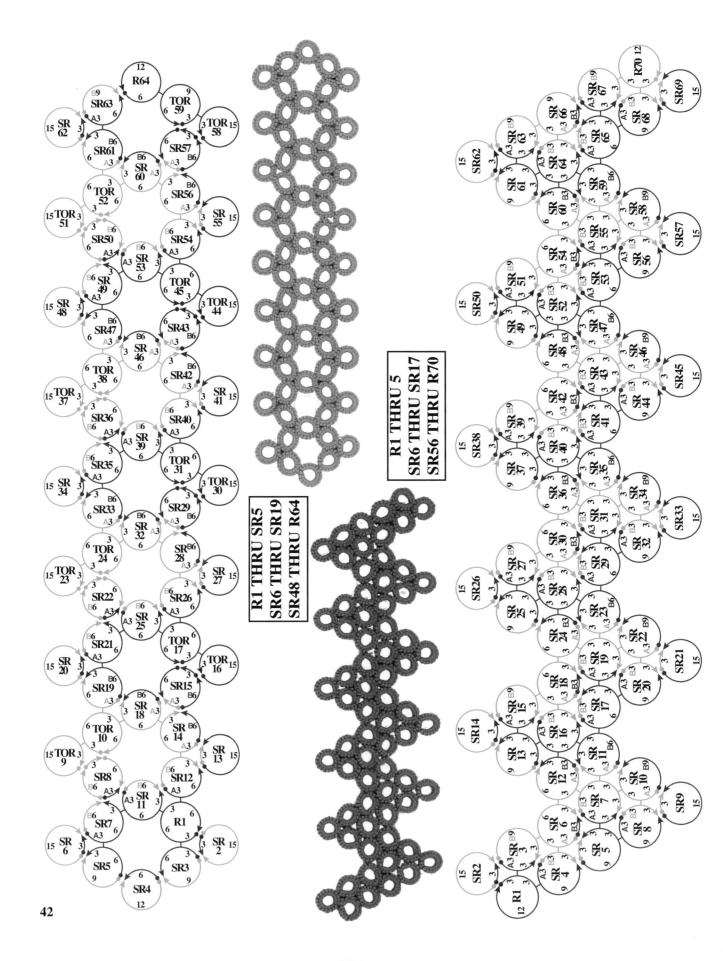

R1 THRU 5
SR6 THRU SR17
SR56 THRU R70

R1 THRU SR5
SR6 THRU SR19
SR48 THRU R64

42

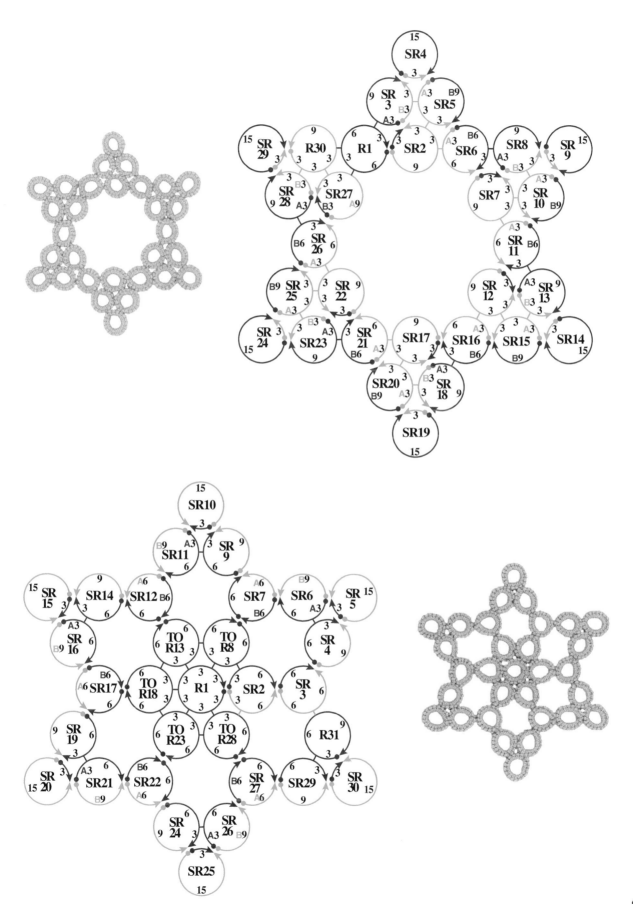

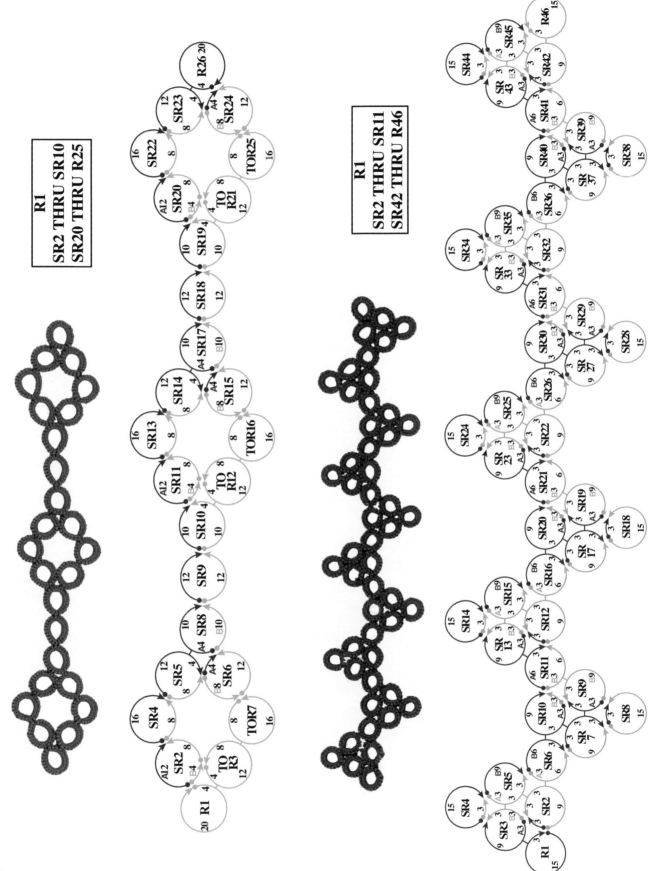

R1
SR2 THRU SR10
SR20 THRU R25

R1
SR2 THRU SR11
SR42 THRU R46

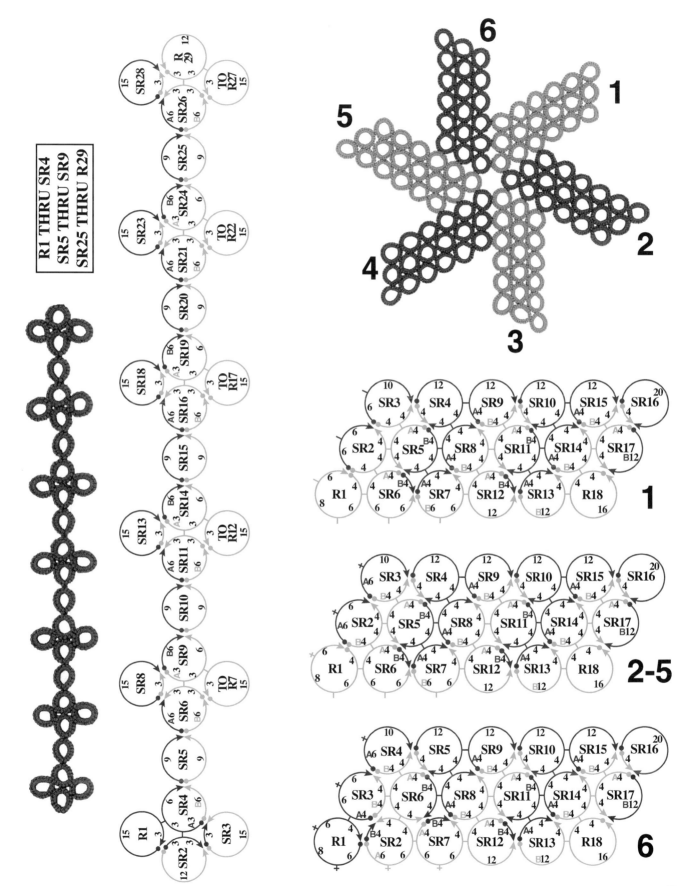

R1 THRU SR4
SR5 THRU SR9
SR25 THRU R29

45

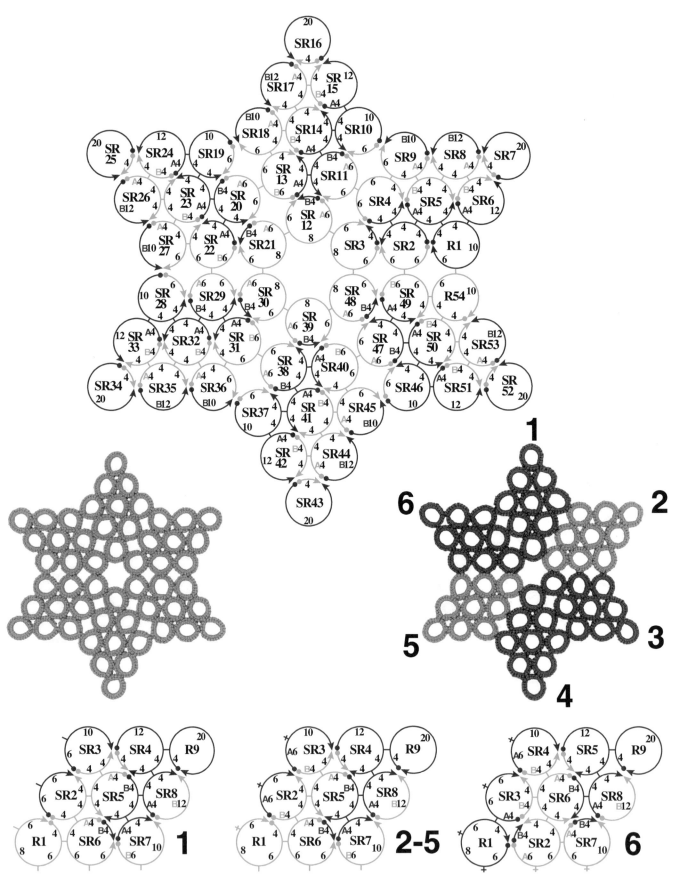

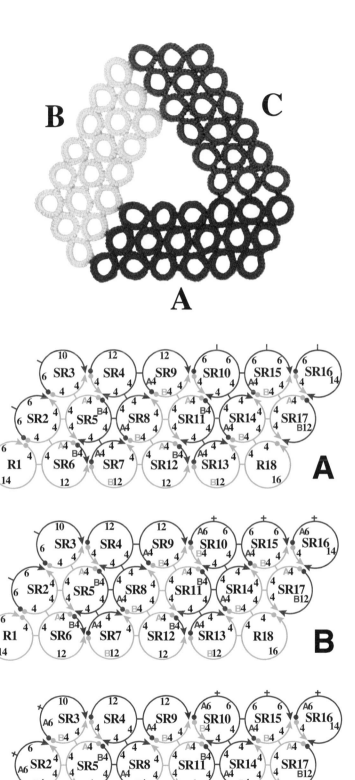

DESIGN IDEAS

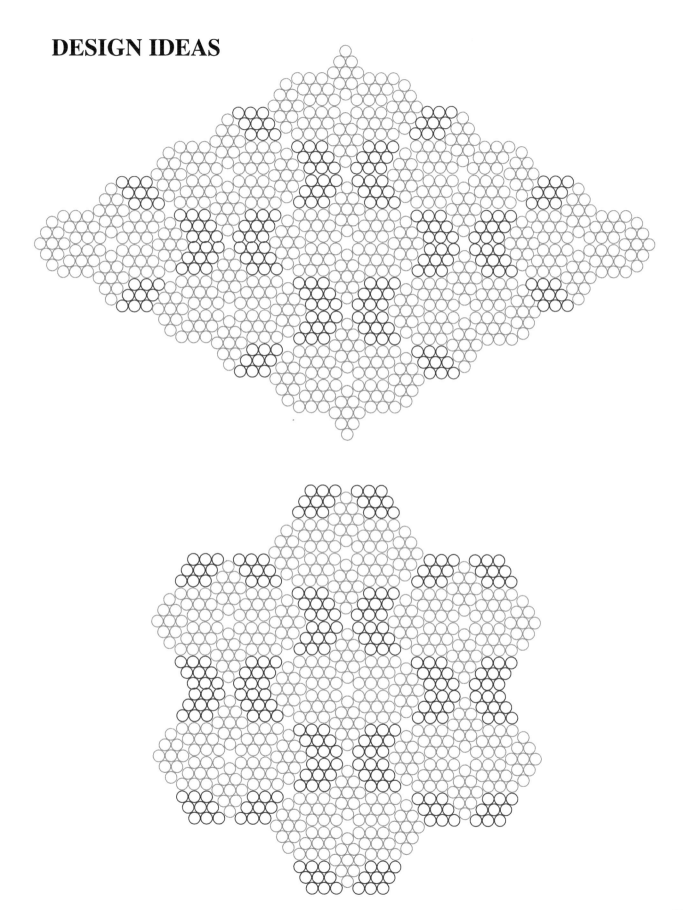

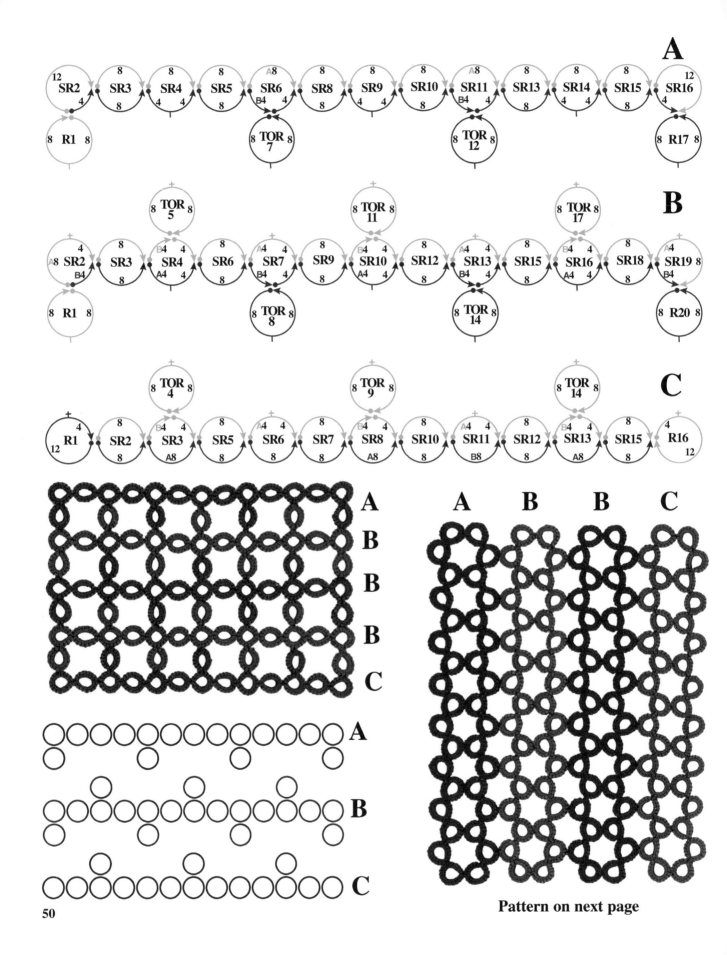

Pattern on next page

50

Row A is the initial base row.
Row B joins to Row A.
Row C is the final row and joins to Row B.

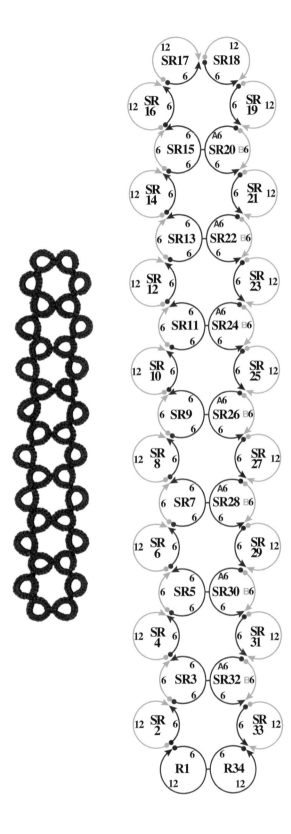

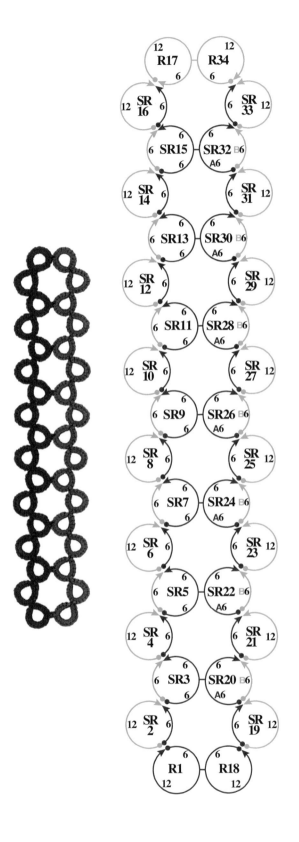

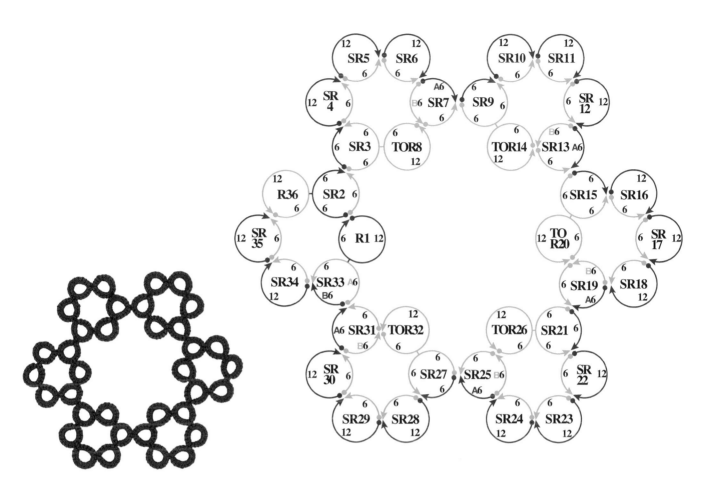

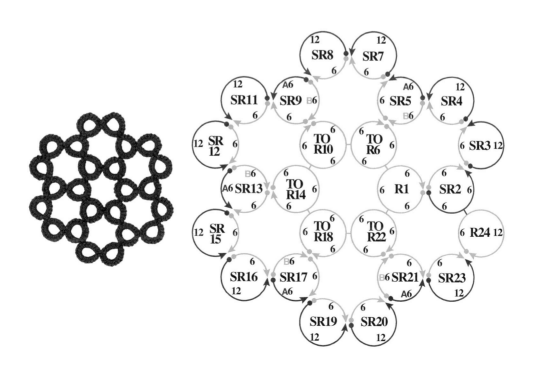

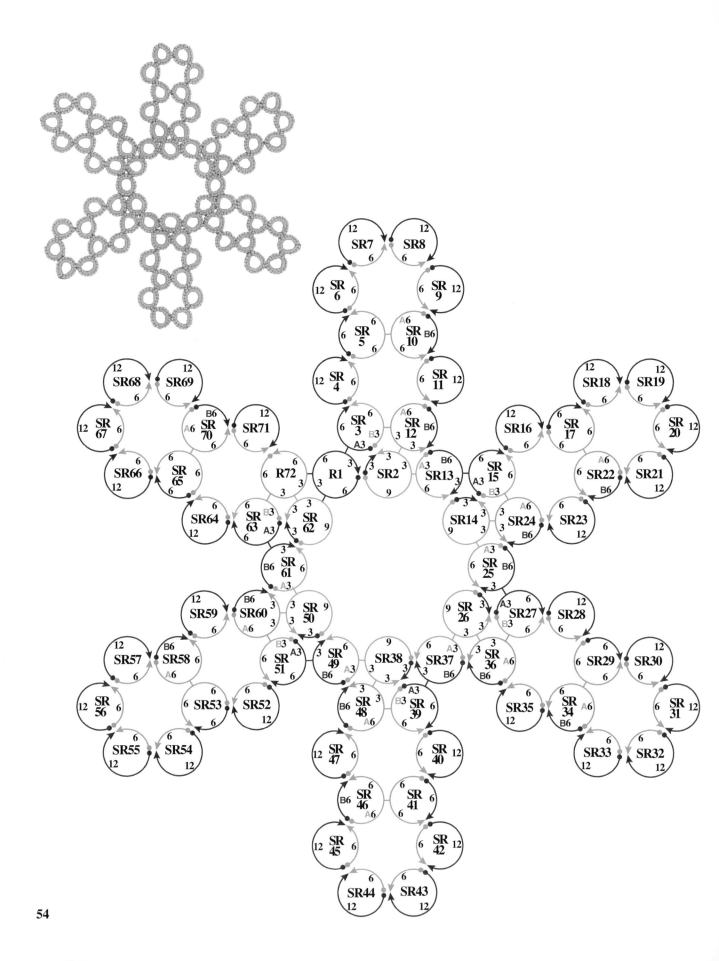

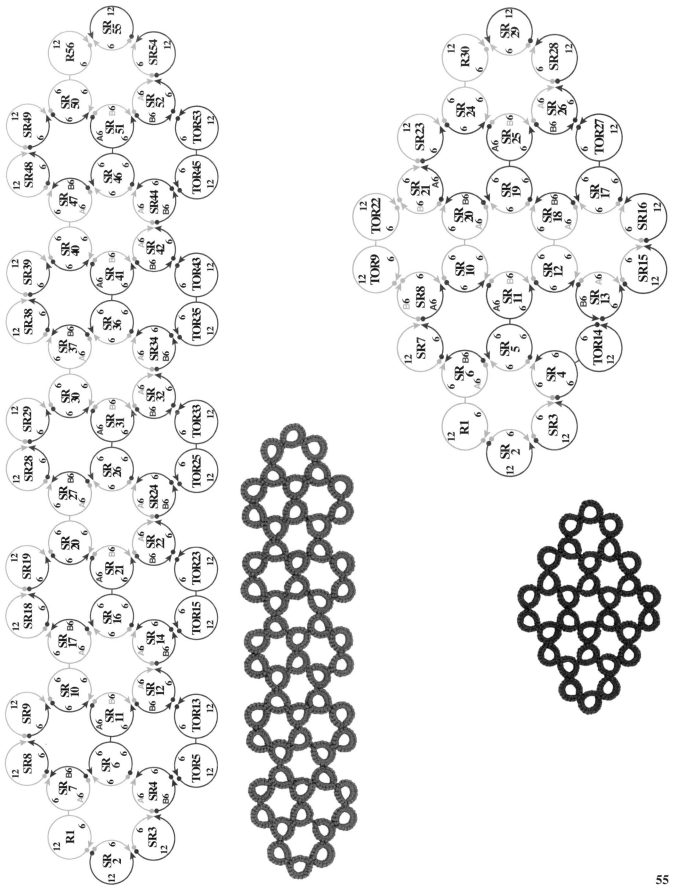

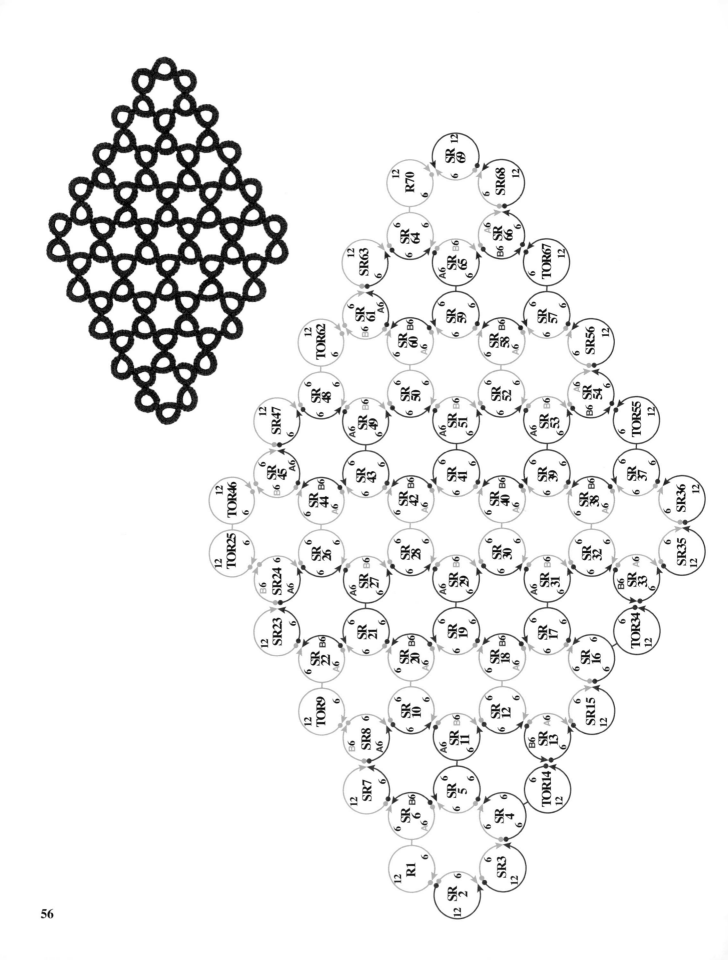

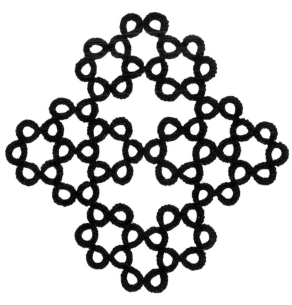

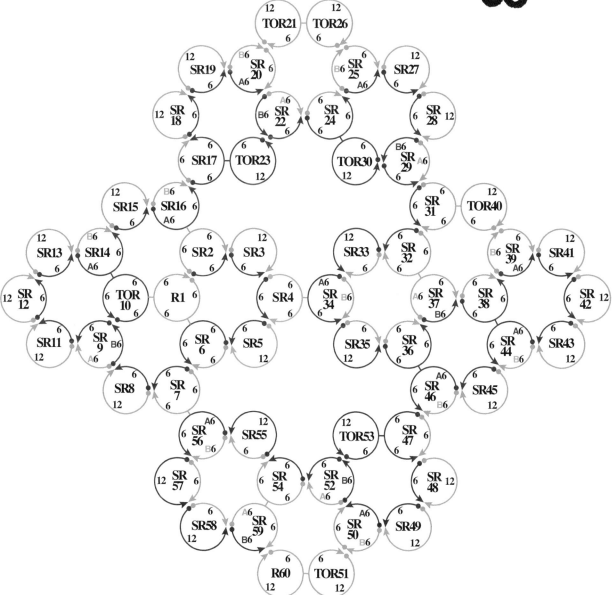

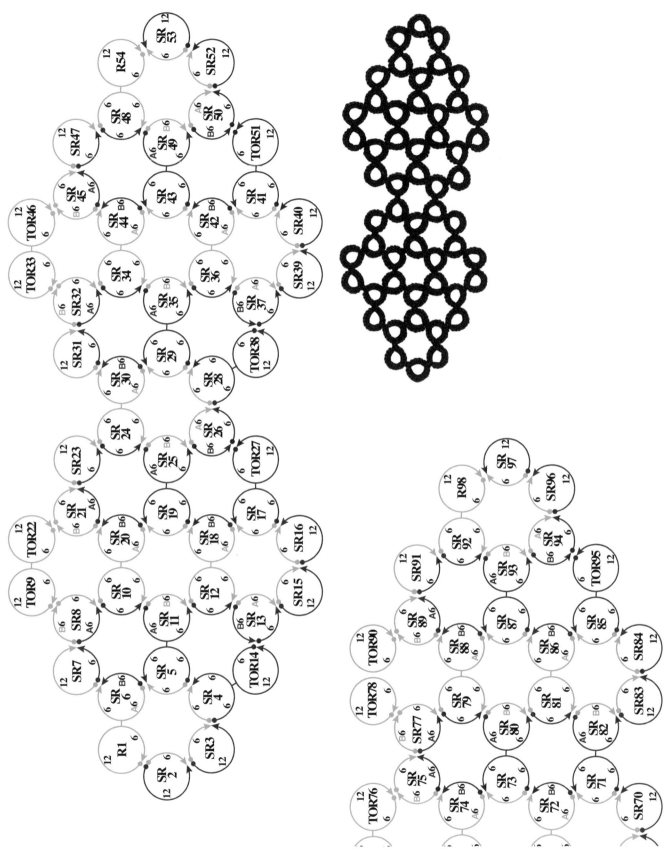

Photo and rest of pattern on next page

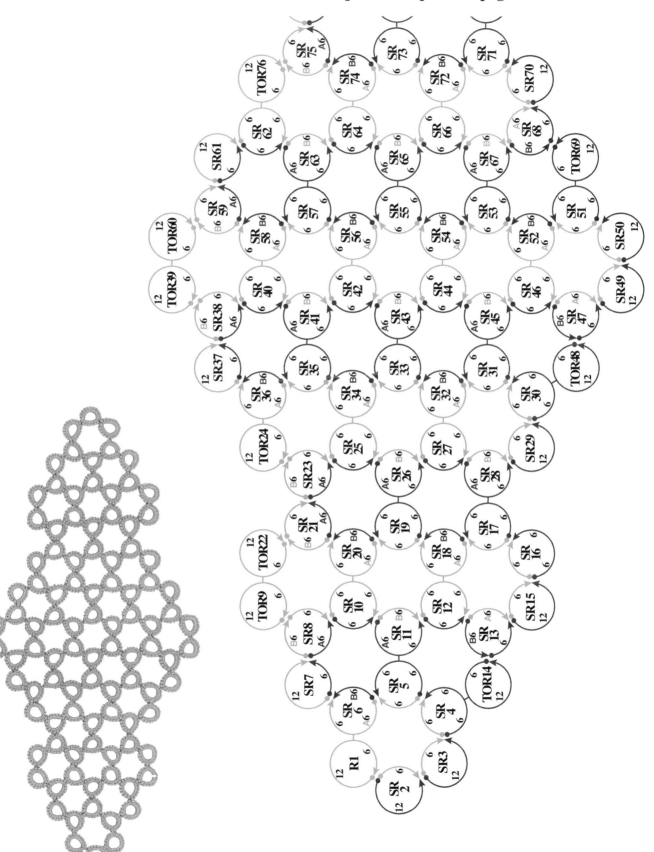

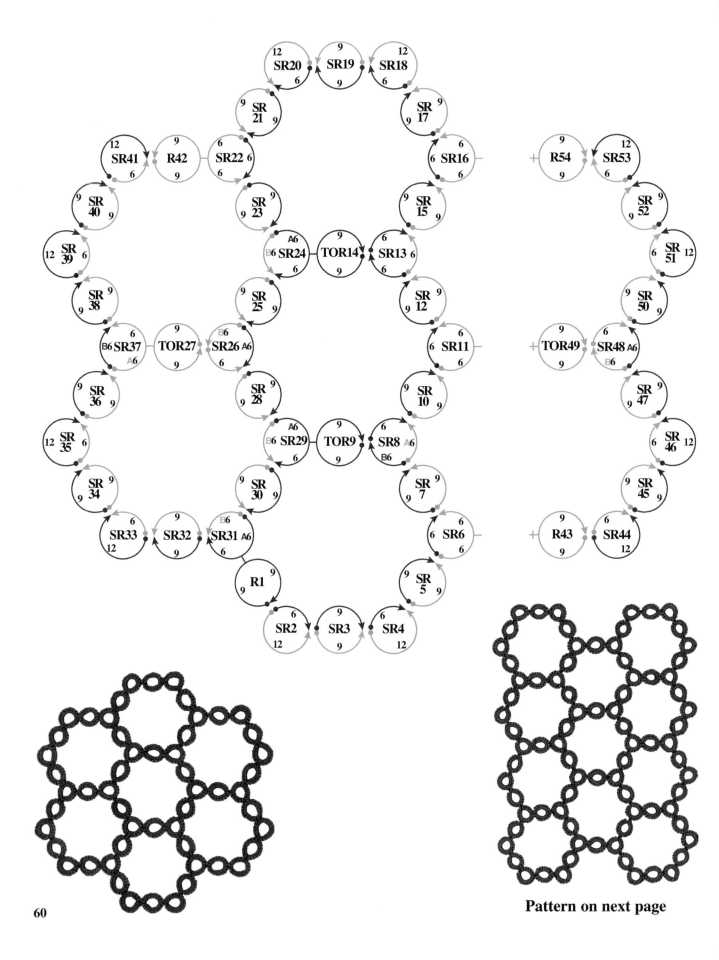

Pattern on next page

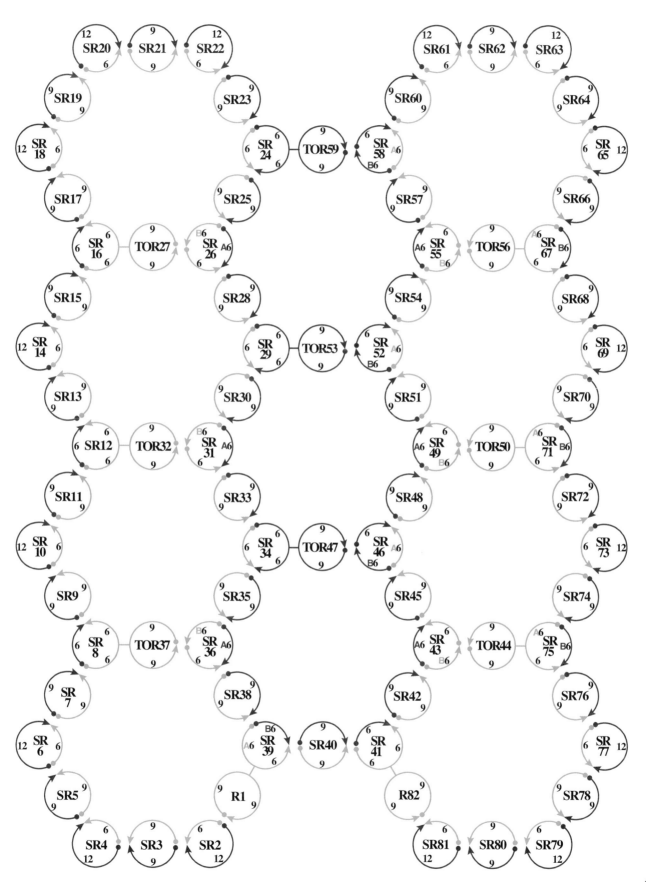

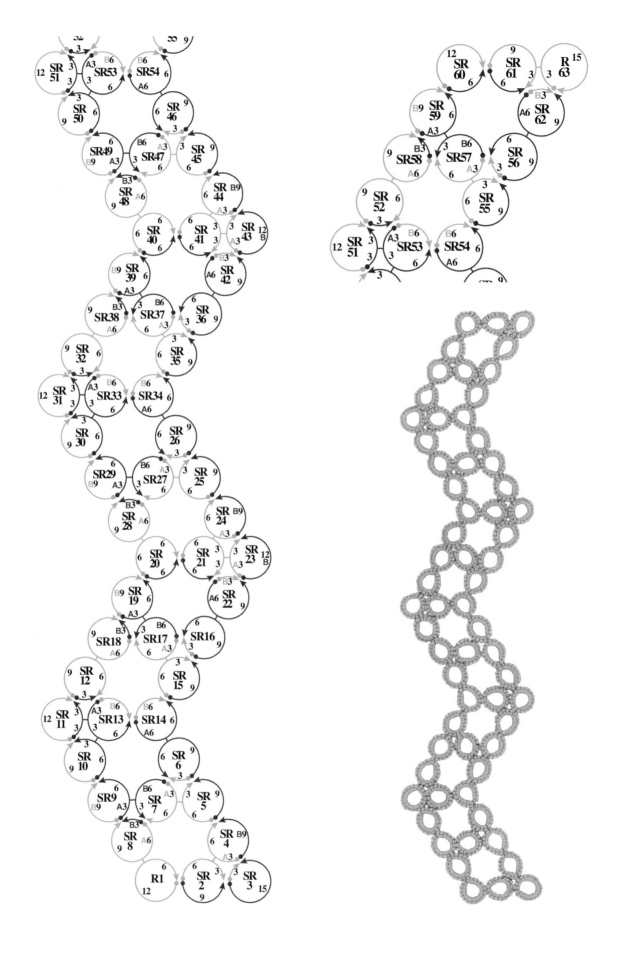

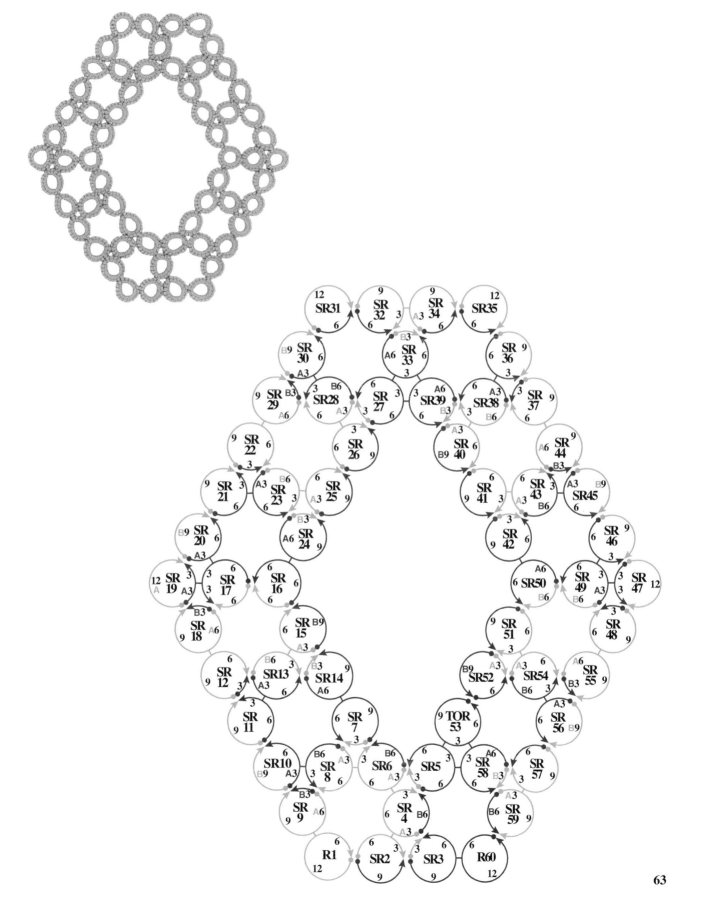

63

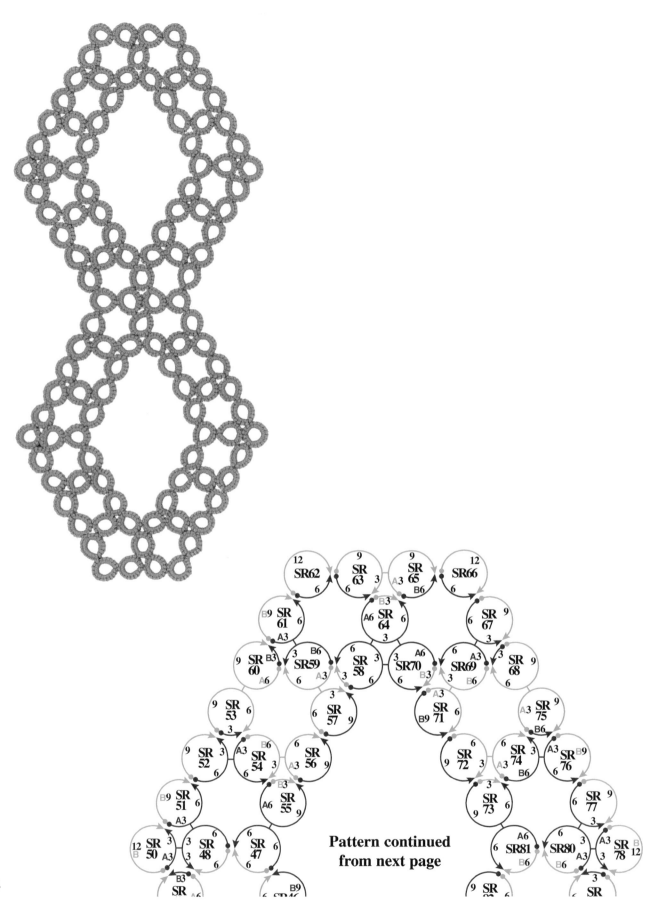

Pattern continued from next page

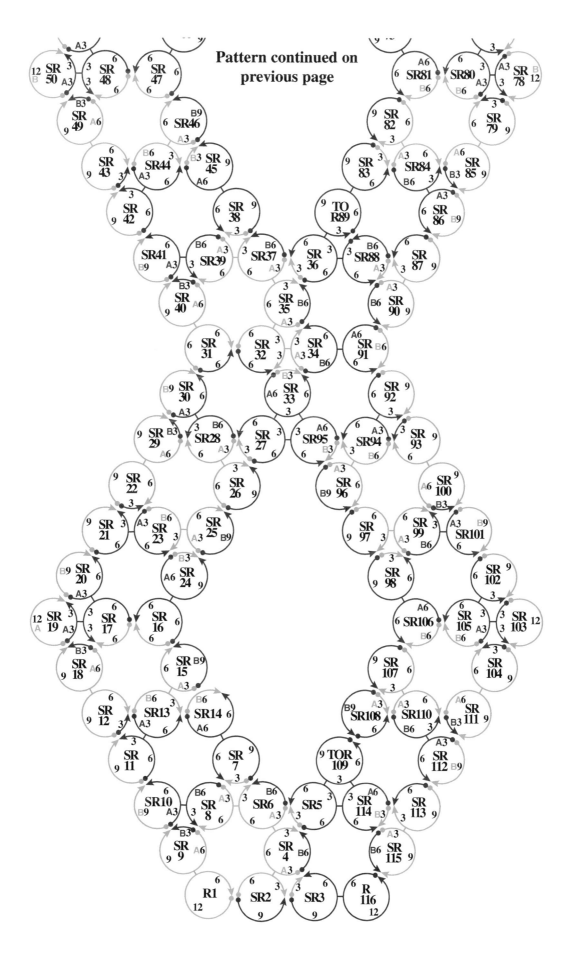

Pattern continued on previous page

Printed in Great Britain
by Amazon.co.uk, Ltd.,
Marston Gate.